EARLY CHILDHOOD EDUCATION SERIES

High-Quality Early Learning for a Changing World: What Educators Need to Know and Do
BEVERLY FALK

Guiding Principles for the New Early Childhood Professional: Building on Strength and Competence
VALORA WASHINGTON & BRENDA GADSON

Leading for Change in Early Care and Education: Cultivating Leadership from Within
ANNE L. DOUGLASS

When Pre-K Comes to School: Policy, Partnerships, and the Early Childhood Education Workforce
BETHANY WILINSKI

Young Investigators: The Project Approach in the Early Years, 3rd Ed.
JUDY HARRIS HELM & LILIAN G. KATZ

Continuity in Children's Worlds: Choices and Consequences for Early Childhood Settings
MELISSA M. JOZWIAK, BETSY J. CAHILL, & RACHEL THEILHEIMER

The Early Intervention Guidebook for Families and Professionals: Partnering for Success, 2nd Ed.
BONNIE KEILTY

STEM Learning with Young Children: Inquiry Teaching with Ramps and Pathways
SHELLY COUNSELL, LAWRENCE ESCALADA, ROSEMARY GEIKEN, MELISSA SANDER, JILL UHLENBERG, BETH VAN MEETEREN, SONIA YOSHIZAWA, & BETTY ZAN

Courageous Leadership in Early Childhood Education: Taking a Stand for Social Justice
SUSI LONG, MARIANA SOUTO-MANNING, & VIVIAN MARIA VASQUEZ, EDS.

Teaching Kindergarten: Learner-Centered Classrooms for the 21st Century
JULIE DIAMOND, BETSY GROB, & FRETTA REITZES, EDS.

Healthy Learners: A Whole Child Approach to Reducing Disparities in Early Education
ROBERT CROSNOE, CLAUDE BONAZZO, & NINA WU

The New Early Childhood Professional: A Step-by-Step Guide to Overcoming Goliath
VALORA WASHINGTON, BRENDA GADSON, & KATHRYN L. AMEL

Eight Essential Techniques for Teaching with Intention: What Makes Reggio and Other Inspired Approaches Effective
ANN LEWIN-BENHAM

Teaching and Learning in a Diverse World, 4th Ed.
PATRICIA G. RAMSEY

In the Spirit of the Studio: Learning from the *Atelier* of Reggio Emilia, 2nd Ed.
LELLA GANDINI, LYNN HILL, LOUISE CADWELL, & CHARLES SCHWALL, EDS.

Leading Anti-Bias Early Childhood Programs: A Guide for Change
LOUISE DERMAN-SPARKS, DEBBIE LEEKEENAN, & JOHN NIMMO

Exploring Mathematics Through Play in the Early Childhood Classroom
AMY NOELLE PARKS

Becoming Young Thinkers: Deep Project Work in the Classroom
JUDY HARRIS HELM

The Early Years Matter: Education, Care, and the Well-Being of Children, Birth to 8
MARILOU HYSON & HEATHER BIGGAR TOMLINSON

Thinking Critically About Environments for Young Children: Bridging Theory and Practice
LISA P. KUH, ED.

Standing Up for Something Every Day: Ethics and Justice in Early Childhood Classrooms
BEATRICE S. FENNIMORE

FirstSchool: Transforming PreK–3rd Grade for African American, Latino, and Low-Income Children
SHARON RITCHIE & LAURA GUTMANN, EDS.

The States of Child Care: Building a Better System
SARA GABLE

Early Childhood Education for a New Era: Leading for Our Profession
STACIE G. GOFFIN

Everyday Artists: Inquiry and Creativity in the Early Childhood Classroom
DANA FRANTZ BENTLEY

Multicultural Teaching in the Early Childhood Classroom: Approaches, Strategies, and Tools, Preschool–2nd Grade
MARIANA SOUTO-MANNING

Inclusion in the Early Childhood Classroom: What Makes a Difference?
SUSAN L. RECCHIA & YOON-JOO LEE

To look for other titles in this series, visit www.tcpress.com

continued

Language Building Blocks
Anita Pandey

Understanding the Language Development and Early Education of Hispanic Children
Eugene E. García & Erminda H. García

Moral Classrooms, Moral Children, 2nd Ed.
Rheta DeVries & Betty Zan

Defending Childhood
Beverly Falk, Ed.

Don't Leave the Story in the Book
Mary Hynes-Berry

Starting with Their Strengths
Deborah C. Lickey & Denise J. Powers

The Play's the Thing
Elizabeth Jones & Gretchen Reynolds

Twelve Best Practices for Early Childhood Education
Ann Lewin-Benham

Big Science for Growing Minds
Jacqueline Grennon Brooks

What If All the Kids Are White? 2nd Ed.
Louise Derman-Sparks & Patricia G. Ramsey

Seen and Heard
Ellen Lynn Hall & Jennifer Kofkin Rudkin

Supporting Boys' Learning
Barbara Sprung, Merle Froschl, & Nancy Gropper

Young English Language Learners
Eugene E. García & Ellen C. Frede, Eds.

Connecting Emergent Curriculum and Standards in the Early Childhood Classroom
Sydney L. Schwartz & Sherry M. Copeland

Infants and Toddlers at Work
Ann Lewin-Benham

The View from the Little Chair in the Corner
Cindy Rzasa Bess

Culture and Child Development in Early Childhood Programs
Carollee Howes

The Story in the Picture
Christine Mulcahey

Educating and Caring for Very Young Children, 2nd Ed.
Doris Bergen, Rebecca Reid, & Louis Torelli

Beginning School
Richard M. Clifford & Gisele M. Crawford, Eds.

Emergent Curriculum in the Primary Classroom
Carol Anne Wien, Ed.

Enthusiastic and Engaged Learners
Marilou Hyson

Powerful Children
Ann Lewin-Benham

The Early Care and Education Teaching Workforce at the Fulcrum
Sharon Lynn Kagan, Kristie Kauerz, & Kate Tarrant

Windows on Learning, 2nd Ed.
Judy Harris Helm, Sallee Beneke, & Kathy Steinheimer

Ready or Not
Stacie G. Goffin & Valora Washington

Supervision in Early Childhood Education, 3rd Ed.
Joseph J. Caruso with M. Temple Fawcett

Guiding Children's Behavior
Eileen S. Flicker & Janet Andron Hoffman

The War Play Dilemma, 2nd Ed.
Diane E. Levin & Nancy Carlsson-Paige

Possible Schools
Ann Lewin-Benham

Everyday Goodbyes
Nancy Balaban

Playing to Get Smart
Elizabeth Jones & Renatta M. Cooper

How to Work with Standards in the Early Childhood Classroom
Carol Seefeldt

Understanding Assessment and Evaluation in Early Childhood Education, 2nd Ed.
Dominic F. Gullo

The Emotional Development of Young Children, 2nd Ed.
Marilou Hyson

Effective Partnering for School Change
Jie-Qi Chen et al.

Young Children Continue to Reinvent Arithmetic—2nd Grade, 2nd Ed.
Constance Kamii

Bringing Learning to Life
Louise Boyd Cadwell

The Colors of Learning
Rosemary Althouse, Margaret H. Johnson, & Sharon T. Mitchell

A Matter of Trust
Carollee Howes & Sharon Ritchie

Embracing Identities in Early Childhood Education
Susan Grieshaber & Gaile S. Cannella, Eds.

Bambini: The Italian Approach to Infant/Toddler Care
Lella Gandini & Carolyn Pope Edwards, Eds.

Serious Players in the Primary Classroom, 2nd Ed.
Selma Wassermann

Young Children Reinvent Arithmetic, 2nd Ed.
Constance Kamii

Bringing Reggio Emilia Home
Louise Boyd Cadwell

HIGH-QUALITY EARLY LEARNING FOR A CHANGING WORLD

What Educators Need to Know and Do

BEVERLY FALK

Foreword by Jacqueline Jones

TEACHERS COLLEGE PRESS
TEACHERS COLLEGE | COLUMBIA UNIVERSITY
NEW YORK AND LONDON

Published by Teachers College Press, 1234 Amsterdam Avenue, New York, NY 10027

Figures 2.6, 2.9, 6.1, 6.2, 6.3, 6.4, 6.5, 6.6, 6.7, 9.1, 9.2, 11.1, 11.2, 11.3, 11.4, 11.5, 15.1, 16.1, and 16.2 photographed by Meryl Feigenberg. Figures 7.3 , 8.1, 8.2, and 8.3 photographed by Emma Markarian. Used with permission.

Chapter 15 contains a poem excerpted from the book *Children Learn What They Live*, by Dorothy Law Nolte and Rachel Harris. Copyright © 1998 by Dorothy Law Nolte and Rachel Harris. The poem "Children Learn What They Live" copyright © 1972 by Dorothy Law Nolte. Used by permission of Workman Publishing Co., Inc., New York. All rights reserved.

Chapter 18 contains an excerpt rom a homily written by Bishop Ken Untener in 1979. Used by permission of Little Books of the Diocese of Saginaw, Saginaw, MI.

Library of Congress Cataloging-in-Publication Data is available at loc.gov

ISBN 978-0-8077-5940-0 (paper)
ISBN 978-0-8077-7693-3 (ebook)

Printed on acid-free paper
Manufactured in the United States of America

25 24 23 22 21 20 19 18 8 7 6 5 4 3 2 1

This book is dedicated to all the caregivers and teachers of young children who heroically do the critically important yet frequently undervalued work of nurturing the foundation for lifelong learning.

Contents

PART II: LEARNING, CURRICULUM, AND ASSESSMENT

Foreword

Providing all children with high-quality early learning experiences is the goal of every early childhood educator. However, it is not always clear what the practices and settings that define *high quality* actually look like. Our discourse often assumes an "I'll know it when I see it" attitude. Yet if our work is going to reduce or eliminate the opportunity/achievement gaps and ensure a solid foundation from which all children can reach their full potential, high quality must be more than a theoretical notion. In *High-Quality Early Learning for a Changing World: What Educators Need to Know and Do*, Professor Falk opens a window into a world of high-quality professional practice that not only is aspirational but is being operationalized by real teachers in very real-world settings.

Our often-well-intended attempts to lessen ethnic, racial, linguistic, and socioeconomic disparities in educational achievement have frequently placed an overreliance on test scores, strategies to expedite learning, teacher-proof curricula, and the infamous "drill-and-kill" approach to teaching. Falk, however, argues that children who are most likely to face academic underachievement deserve the same types of exploratory, inquiry-based, active learning experiences that their higher-resourced peers enjoy. Respecting young children's families and communities, their experiences, and their own interests is at the core of an instructional practice that walks with the child—guiding and scaffolding early learning experiences that, in the words of the mission of the Foundation for Child Development,

- affirm their individual, family, and community assets;
- fortify them against harmful consequences arising from economic instability and social exclusion; and
- strengthen their developmental potential.

Grounding her pedagogical perspective in the science of early development, Falk presents an up-close and personal window into the teaching practices of five extraordinary early childhood teachers across preschool through 2nd grade. Rather than relying on hypothetical examples of good practice that represent sound early childhood theory, Falk takes the reader deep into the theory and practice of successful real-life early childhood teachers. The divide between early childhood education and "schools" is bridged artfully and skillfully as we view these five professionals in action as each of them demonstrates a keen understanding of how children learn and the practices that facilitate and promote optimal development.

Divided into three sections—(1) Foundational Knowledge to Guide Teaching; (2) Learning, Curriculum, and Assessment; and (3) Strategies for Supporting Children's Learning—we see theory and practice interwoven as the reader is guided across the multiple aspects of high-quality early childhood education. Falk does not just provide a set of activities. Rather, there is a clear rationale for the teachers' actions, the arrangement of the classroom, the materials, and the activities. For example, the goal is not simply to have a lot of stuff in the classroom; materials should be purposeful and able to invite inquiry and exploration from a range of developmental levels. There is no room for random activities. Teachers are intentional about the types of activities that are provided, know how they can be offered in a manner that is predictable for young children, and implement the strategies to ensure that transitions and routines can help the day flow in a well-managed and smooth manner.

In high-quality environments, early learning standards and developmentally appropriate practices are not mutually exclusive. Falk situates standards in the context of an inquiry-based environment that is conducive to children's learning and appropriate to individual levels of development. Nor are these settings in which teachers fear assessment. Rather, these professionals know that collecting information about children's learning and development is essential. They are curious about how children are making sense of the world, and they work to improve their own powers of observation and documentation in order to make more informed instructional decisions.

Professor Falk is also keenly aware that the child's family plays a critical role as an educational partner with the teacher. Connecting with the parents and gaining a real understanding of the context of the culture and family in which the child lives is also part of building high-quality experiences for young children.

The descriptions of high-quality early learning settings are a delight to read; these are the classrooms and teachers that we want every child to encounter. However, we must always acknowledge that creating and managing these joyful environments is the work of skilled professionals who are constantly striving to raise their levels of expertise even higher. They understand human development, especially in its very early stages, and they marry that knowledge with the art of embracing families and creating respectful, curious, and confident communities of learners. This is work that requires mastery of competences and ongoing professional learning, and it does not end with an AA, BA, or MA degree.

Professor Falk gives us much more than a guidebook to building high-quality early learning environments. This text is a portrait of what it means to be an early childhood professional and to take seriously the job of establishing meaningful relationships with children, families, and other professional colleagues. It is these relationships that will shape the social, emotional, and cognitive foundations of generations of productive and enlightened citizens. No work is more important.

—Jacqueline Jones
President and CEO, Foundation for Child Development

Acknowledgments

As with all milestones in life, this project could not have been accomplished without the support and influence of many—my funders, collaborators, colleagues and thought-partners, friends, and loved ones.

Thank you to the Foundation for Child Development—especially Foundation president Jacqueline Jones and program officer Sara Vecchiotti—for funding the High-Quality Early Learning Project, which made possible the case studies of teachers who are featured in this book.

I am also immensely grateful to Meryl Feigenberg, my collaborator and videographer for this project, whose artistry in shaping the videos for the collection so beautifully highlighted the nuances of responsive, child-centered teaching and lent insight to the writing of this book.

Additionally, I am deeply grateful for having had the opportunity to learn from the masterful New York City teachers featured in the pages to follow—Yvonne Smith (prekindergarten teacher at Central Park East 1 Elementary School in East Harlem); Fanny Roman (kindergarten teacher at PS 244Q—The Active Learning School in Flushing, Queens); Jessica Lawrence and Andrene Robinson (1st-grade teachers at the Bronx Community Charter School); Kimberly Fritschy and Vanessa Keller (1st/2nd-grade teachers at the Earth School, Lower East Side), and Emma Markarian (prekindergarten coordinator, Tweed Courthouse, Lower Manhattan). By so generously sharing their work and their knowledge for the video and written case studies featured here, many of which can be found at highqualityearlylearning.org, these teachers make visible the power of research informed by practice.

The Foundation for Child Development has also supported another project in which I am involved—an examination of high-quality teaching in culturally and linguistically diverse communities—that has made it possible to learn from others in the field and has influenced the ideas shared here. In relation to that project, I acknowledge my appreciation for my coprincipal investigator, Mariana Souto-Manning, and our research team—Nancy Cardwell, Dina López, Ayesha Rabadi-Raol, Livia Galvani de Barros Cruz, Elizabeth Rollins, Nicole McGowan, Hyeyoung Kim, Aura Perez, Patricia Godoy, and Nancy Bradt—for the exchange of ideas we have had on this important work.

A big thank you goes to Nancy Gropper and Rima Shore, my writing and thought partners for the document produced for the *Joining with the Learner* gathering held in New York City in 2016, which also helped to clarify many of the ideas shared in this book (Falk, Gropper, & Shore, 2017). In addition, I appreciate my many other New York City early childhood colleagues with whom I have participated in conversations and projects to better serve the young children and families in our city. A special shout-out to my friends Renee Dinnerstein, Betsy Grob, and Fretta Reitzes, who have facilitated the sharing of my work and whose mentoring has touched the lives of so many early childhood teachers.

Thank you also to Teachers College Press, for providing me with the opportunity to make this book possible, especially Sarah Biondello and John Bylander, the editors of my project, for the support, patience, and helpful suggestions that have helped me to strengthen this text.

And finally, I thank my primary circle—Alan, Meryl, Luba, Thabiti, Anaiya, and Asa—whose love continually nourishes me and inspires my hopes for the future.

Introduction

Today there is evidence from multiple disciplines that early childhood is *the* most important time for the development of lifelong human capacities (Shonkoff & Phillips, 2000), that the quality of early experiences in early education is a critical factor affecting a child's life trajectory (Barnett, 1995; Pianta & Walsh, 2014), and that supporting children and families during the early childhood years is the best investment a society can make (Elango, García, Heckman, & Hojman, 2015; García, Heckman, Leaf, & Prados, 2017; Heckman, 2012; Heckman, Pinto, & Savelyev, 2013). Growing awareness of these facts about the early years of life has led to new investments in early childhood programs. This expansion is also fueled by our nation's desire to prepare young children for the skills they will need as citizens of our future society. It is also driven by the commitment of many to make progress on providing more equitable opportunities for children and families from low-income and racially, culturally, and linguistically diverse backgrounds who historically have been underserved by schools and other societal institutions (García & Frede, 2010; Ladson-Billings, 2006; Valdés, 1996).

PURPOSES

In recognition of these changing dynamics, this book aims to shed light on teaching practices, classroom environments, and family involvement practices that support young children and their families to develop and thrive in our increasingly complex world. Based on a rapidly growing body of research from multiple disciplines, including cognitive and developmental psychology, neuroscience, educational pedagogy, language and cultural studies, social science, and economics, as well as my own 40-plus years' experience as an early childhood educator, it offers a guide for how to create "high-quality early learning," defining this as active, engaging, and enriching experiences that nurture cognitive skills (critical thinking and problem solving) as well as social/emotional and cultural/linguistic development (Falk, 2012; Genishi & Dyson, 2009; Hakuta & Garcia, 1989; National Association for the Education of Young Children [NAEYC], 2009). In acknowledgment of the rapidly increasing diversity of our population and the historic educational debt (Ladson-Billings, 2006) owed to so many who have been the recipients of inequitable opportunities, I particularly emphasize practices that are responsive to and sustaining for children and families from minoritized communities.

THE STATE OF EARLY CHILDHOOD TODAY

Today, more than ever before, a quality education is essential for the survival of all citizens. The notion of quality must now take into consideration a range of societal changes: the fact that knowledge is exploding exponentially, that demographics are increasingly diverse, that rapid technological advances are impacting every aspect of our lives, that job opportunities are shifting away from low-level skills toward high-level skills, that we are living in a global economy where power and politics can be dangerous and complex, that the sustenance of our democracy demands informed and committed citizen action, that the need for all adults in a family to work creates ever-pressing needs for child care. Overall, there is an increasing demand for citizens who can think critically, understand and analyze complexities, identify problems, imagine and create to solve problems, and be innovative as well as adaptive to rapidly changing conditions and contexts (Darling-Hammond, 2010; Falk, 2012).

A popular response to these societal changes has been to look to schools to better educate our future citizens, emphasizing more challenging standards, measured by tests. In the early childhood arena, this is evident in the increased focus on academic skills that is proliferating in the younger grades (Bassok, Latham, & Rorem, 2016; Gao, 2005). Out of a belief that early introduction of academic instruction will better prepare young children for the challenging standards they will have to meet in later grades, teachers in settings for younger and younger children are increasingly emphasizing symbols and skills, despite the fact that many children of this age may not yet have developed a capacity to comprehend these kinds of abstractions (Elkind, 2001; Fuller, Bein, Bridges, Kim, & Rabe-Hesketh, 2017).

And thus active, play-based experiences such as block play, dramatic play, work with manipulative materials, investigations of sand and water and other scientific phenomena, cooking, art, writing, music and movement, storytime, trips, even rest time and recess, are fast disappearing from classrooms for young children (Miller & Almon, 2009). These are being replaced by an increased emphasis on paper-and-pencil work. This transformation is happening everywhere, but it is especially prevalent in schools that serve low-income and minoritized populations, where it is often assumed that greater time spent on test prep will help to ensure that "those children" will not lag behind their more well-resourced peers (Nichols, Glass, & Berliner, 2006). However, everything we know about how children learn suggests that depriving them of active, play-based experiences is harmful—for academic as well as social/emotional reasons (National Association for the Education of Young Children & National Association for Early Childhood Specialists in State Departments of Education, 2003). As the American Academy of Pediatrics has warned, "free and unstructured play is not only healthy, but essential for helping children reach important social, emotional, and cognitive developmental milestones as well as helping them manage stress and become resilient" (Ginsberg, 2007).

The issues presented in this brief introduction are discussed in greater detail in the remainder of this book. The aim is to help you, the reader, understand how young children learn, how to intentionally teach in ways that support how young children learn, and what educators need to do to balance the demands of high-quality, developmentally appropriate teaching with perceived current societal challenges and demands.

OVERVIEW OF THE BOOK

Part I, "Foundational Knowledge to Guide Teaching," begins with a discussion of foundations to guide early childhood teaching. Chapter 1 presents an overview of the research about learning and development. Referencing understandings from multiple disciplines, it offers implications for how to teach in ways that support how young children learn.

Chapter 2 details how to organize the classroom as a learning environment. The physical environment—activity areas that support children's learning, how these should be arranged, what materials should be in them and how they should be stored, and how these areas can be used to support different kinds of learning—is described and explained.

Chapter 3 describes routines, schedules, and transitions throughout the day—critical elements of a classroom that enable productive learning.

Chapter 4 speaks to the importance of understanding the context in which you teach in order to effectively connect with children and their families. Guidance is offered about how to get to know the school and community in which you teach, how to understand the cultural contexts of your learners, and how to learn about the strengths and needs of each learner.

Part II, "Learning, Curriculum, and Assessment," focuses on how to support children's learning through active experiences, how to use and develop curriculum, and how to assess children's progress. Chapter 5 addresses how to connect play, purposes, and standards/goals. Referencing the research on the importance of active learning, it discusses the balance that teachers need to find between play, explicit instruction, and the standards required by districts and states. How children learn through explorations in classroom centers and through explicit instruction is examined.

Chapter 6 presents images of how children's learning is nurtured through child-directed, center-based work and teacher-facilitated inquiry in a kindergarten classroom.

Chapter 7 discusses learning through interdisciplinary curriculum studies. The challenges and benefits of designing your own studies versus using predesigned curricula are addressed.

Chapter 8 describes a prekindergarten classroom that focuses on the needs and interests of the learners in the context of carrying out a required curriculum.

Chapter 9 depicts a teacher-created curriculum in a prekindergarten class that is grounded in knowledge of how young children learn and in the questions and interests of the learners.

Chapter 10 focuses on how assessment can inform teaching and support learning. It reviews the different kinds of evidence that teachers can collect to keep track of what children know and can do, their different approaches to learning, their strengths, and their needs. It offers suggestions for how to work with required standards without abandoning principles of developmentally appropriate teaching and how to share information about children's learning with families, administrators, and the children themselves.

Chapter 11 presents a whole-class study of a 1st-grade classroom that is guided by teachers' assessments of the children's interests and understandings. It describes a culminating experience of the study—a museum—that shares what the children have learned with their families and other members of the school community.

Part III, "Strategies for Supporting Children's Learning," delves into teaching strategies and other elements of schooling that are essential to high-quality early learning environments. Chapter 12 focuses on a developmental approach to literacy learning. Suggestions are offered

for providing supports to children at different points along the developmental continuum. Also discussed is how to balance explicit instruction with intentional guidance and independent play-based activities.

Chapter 13 focuses on deepening children's learning through an inquiry approach to teaching. Beginning with a discussion of purposes for teaching and how to align teaching with chosen purposes, it offers strategies for and examples of how teachers can nurture children to find their own purposes to learn, inquire, pose problems, and think critically and creatively.

Chapter 14 discusses some basic principles for supporting and celebrating the diversity of the children and families in your classroom. It examines how to craft teaching strategies and supports that build on children's strengths and cultural assets; are responsive, relevant, and sustaining to their diversity; honor differences; encourage critical and creative thinking; and demonstrate a belief that all can learn.

Chapter 15 considers what it means to create a community of care as well as the importance of building relationships and supporting all aspects of the child—the social, emotional, physical, cognitive, and cultural self. Strategies for how to do this are addressed.

Chapter 16 describes a 1st/2nd-grade classroom that has many community-building structures and processes in place. Details of how these work offer a guide to how to establish a community of care.

Chapter 17 reviews ways to partner with families in classroom and school life. Among the topics discussed are how to communicate with families and communities about what is going on in the curriculum, how to explain to them the teaching strategies being used in the classroom, how to engage families in supporting children's learning both inside and outside of school, how to give guidance for helping children with homework, and how to collaborate with families to infuse cultural and community assets into the curriculum.

Chapter 18 reflects on what it means to sustain a life in teaching. Framing the teaching life as a "learning life," this chapter concludes the volume by offering strategies for how to manage the inevitable problems and tensions that arise in schools and how to create a community of learners within your classroom and among your colleagues.

As you read through the pages to follow, I hope the ideas presented here provide you with information that you find useful and that will nourish and enrich your own educational life.

Part I

FOUNDATIONAL KNOWLEDGE TO GUIDE TEACHING

CHAPTER 1

Insights from Research on How Children Learn

Over the last several decades, an explosion of research from multiple disciplines has deepened understandings of how young children learn. What we now know for sure is that young children's optimal development is best supported when we pay attention not only to their cognitive development but to their social and emotional development as well. We also know that cognitive development is supported in young children differently than in older kids: young children are active learners who need lots of experiences with materials and relationships to help them make sense of the world. Only by attending to these two important points—caring for the "whole child" and providing lots of opportunities for children to learn through experience—can we hope to help them attain the challenging skills they will need to be active citizens in our changing world.

WHAT WE KNOW ABOUT HOW YOUNG CHILDREN LEARN

This chapter presents and explains some of the key understandings that have emerged from research in different disciplines about the nature of how young children learn.

Children Learn Through Experience

From developmental psychology we have learned that experience is the trigger that enables children to organize their brains to support the challenges they meet. This means that during the early years of life, young children make sense of new concepts and ideas through active engagement with materials, ideas, and relationships. What adults often refer to as "play"—block play, dramatic play, singing, dancing, painting, drawing, and so on—is really the work that young children do to understand the world (Bowman, Donovan, & Burns, 2001; Copple & Bredekamp, 2009). Educators have theorized about this for some time, but recent developments in brain-based research have added other important dimensions to our knowledge.

Experiences Build the Brain

Neuroscience's more recent brain imaging technologies have added support to these earlier understandings. They have confirmed that active experiences are critical for the development and collaboration of the brain's processing systems. Infants are born literally "wired" to learn; the brain at birth possesses over 100 billion neurons. As a result of experiences during the early years, these neurons connect and intertwine. This happens at the rate of *one million new neural connections per second* for the first 2 to 3 years of life! Connections that are most active are strengthened and stabilized, while those that are least active get weakened and are eventually eliminated (Kaczmarek, 1997). By age 3, 75% of this architecture of the brain is created; by age 5, over 90% is formed (Center on the Developing Child, 2017). In this way, the brain is constructed, building a foundation for the development of life's critical competencies—linguistic, conceptual, ethical, social, emotional, and motor—that influence future capacities to learn.

Executive Functioning Develops Through Active, Play-Based Experiences

Brain imaging also informs us that children's engagement in the active experiences that we call play help to develop the part of the brain that enables them to have what are referred to as "executive functioning" skills. Executive functioning includes the skills of self-control, memory (the ability to hold information and recall it when necessary), and cognitive flexibility (the ability to change and adjust mental effort). All of these skills are essential to learning and have been shown to be critical for school success (Leong & Bodrova, 2012). Some examples of executive functioning skills are the ability to do the following: stay seated and quiet while a teacher is talking, line up with a class and walk to various places without running ahead of the group, wait for a turn, understand that everyone cannot be first at the same time or all the time, stay on task and complete assigned work without being distracted.

Other Positive Outcomes of Active Learning

Linked to executive functioning skills are other positive outcomes. These include increased language and communication skills, increased creativity and problem-solving skills, and increased ability to assume the perspective of others. They also include the ability to engage in critical thinking, to make connections, to take on challenges, and to become engaged, self-directed learners (Brown, 2009; Diamond, Barnett, Thomas, & Munro, 2007; Heckman et al., 2013; Kagan & Lowenstein, 2004; Trentacosta & Izard, 2007; Vygotsky, 1966/1977; Zigler, Singer, & Bishop-Josef, 2004).

Many of these positive outcomes have been found to have long-lasting effects. Long-term studies of children who experience the kind of play-based early learning environments that support enhanced executive functioning skills reveal that these children also develop stronger reading comprehension when they get older, higher test scores at the end of high school, and fewer criminal records, less drug addiction, healthier living, and more success/satisfaction in other life factors than peers who do not experience play-based early schooling (Moffitt et al., 2011; Sesma, Mahone, Levine, Eason, & Cutting, 2009).

Emotional, Cognitive, and Physical Development Are Inextricably Linked

New brain imaging technologies also demonstrate how, during the early years of life, emotional development and physical well-being are inextricably intertwined with cognitive abilities into the architecture of the brain (Damasio, 1994; Hinton, Miyamoto, & della-Chiesa, 2008). Chronic or traumatic experiences—such as prolonged food insecurity and poor health care due to poverty, homelessness, abuse, or neglect—can have severe and long-lasting damaging consequences for the development of children's brains (United Nations, 2006). Additionally, persistent negative factors—such as stress, boredom, confusion, low motivation, and anxiety—can interfere with learning and are also potentially toxic to brain development. This is because when adversity is experienced, heart rate increases, blood pressure rises, and bodies release stress hormones such as adrenaline and cortisol. If this happens repeatedly, over time, increased levels of stress hormones disrupt the development of neural systems involved in regulating learning and memory processes (National Scientific Council on the Developing Child, 2005, 2009, 2010). The internal chemicals produced in response to chronic stressors also exert a "wear-and-tear" effect on the body's health, leading to increased susceptibility to such problems as depression, heart disease, asthma, or diabetes (Danese et al., 2009).

These biological effects of chronic and traumatic experiences can also have corresponding behavioral consequences. Children who experience chronic stress have been found to have difficulties recognizing emotions, adapting to new situations, and forming and maintaining healthy relationships (Gilliam & Shahar, 2006; Pollak, Cicchetti, Hornung, & Reed, 2000).

In contrast, positive emotional interactions and experiences in children's lives—such as the presence of relevance, interest, enjoyment, good relationships, and feelings of safety and self-efficacy—exert a positive impact on learning (Grindal, Hinton, & Shonkoff, 2012). Most importantly, strong, stable, and loving relationships protect against stressors in children's lives and play a critical role in nurturing healthy development (Gunnar, Morison,

Chisholm, & Schuder, 2001; Lally & Mangione, 2017; Nelson & Sheridan, 2011; Pakulak et al., 2017; Shonkoff, 2017).

Young Children's Development Is Naturally Varied

The research is also clear that development in the early years does not proceed in a uniform manner. While all young children are on a similar path of development, they develop at different paces, in different ways, bringing different strengths and intelligences to the learning process (Berger, 2008; Gesell, 1925). Variation and change are the rule rather than the exception (Meisels, 2006). An obvious example is the age at which children learn to walk: Some learn to walk as early as 9 months; some as late as 15 months. This diversity within a developmental span is quite common and normal. For example, we all know that attaining the skill of walking earlier does not make a child a better walker and does not have any lasting beneficial effects. The same is true for other developmental milestones—physical ones such as talking and toileting as well as cognitive/academic ones such as reading (Guddemi, 2013; Suggate, 2012). Each child has his or her own pace on the path of development. Knowing and respecting individual children's paces not only informs efforts to support future growth but actually ensures that optimal growth will occur.

Loving Relationships Support Healthy Development

Research also confirms understandings about the critical role that strong, stable, loving relationships play in nurturing healthy cognitive, social, and emotional development. Social science research reveals that development does not occur in isolation but rather requires supportive environments of caring adults in families, schools, and communities. Studies have found that the quality of relationships that young children experience—ones that provide love, nurturance, and security; that are responsive to children's languages and cultures, foster connections, and encourage engagement and exploration—promote children's optimal development (Hirsh-Pasek, Golinkoff, Berk, & Singer, 2009; Lally & Mangione, 2017; National Scientific Council on the Developing Child, 2004, 2007; Nieto & Bode, 2012; Pakulak et al., 2017; Shonkoff, 2017). When children do not have such a nurturing environment, their development can be seriously disrupted (Polakow, 2012).

Cultural and Community Assets Are Central to Supporting Learning

From research on culture and language we also know that family literacies, funds of knowledge, and community resources are central to quality early learning (García & Frede, 2010; Gay, 2002, 2010; Ladson-Billings, 1995, 2005; Moll, Amanti, Neff, & Gonzalez, 1992; Valdés, 1996). These are critical for bridging children's and families' realities, experiences, and expertise with school-based learning standards, goals, and objectives (Souto-Manning, 2013; Souto-Manning et al., in press).

Even the amount and quality of talk experienced by young children has an impact on their development—in regard not only to learning to read but to their overall intellectual and emotional development. Long-term studies inform us that the more young children engage in quality language exchanges with adults—regardless of the language they speak—the better academic, and social-emotional, success they experience in later years (Hart & Risley, 1995; Ravachew, 2010; Snow, 1983; Snow, Burns, & Griffin, 1998).

QUALITY EARLY EDUCATION AND CARE: TURNING KNOWLEDGE INTO ACTION

The research is unequivocally clear that the ways in which young children grow and learn are naturally varied (earlier is not necessarily better); are grounded in experiential learning; are enhanced by the nurturing of adults who are responsive to and supportive of children's whole being—their physical, social/emotional, and cognitive selves (Akers, 2014); and are supported by practices that are responsive, relevant, and sustaining to their cultural and linguistic backgrounds. Research also confirms that opportunities for active learning, along with supportive and responsive relationships with adults, enhance the development of executive functioning skills, which heighten abilities to handle emotions, develop literacy skills, be creative, and engage successfully in other cognitive functioning.

Given these understandings, the best way to support children's optimal development and to prepare them for the challenges of our changing world is to provide them in the early years with teaching that supports the unique ways in which they learn—lots of opportunities for active involvement in the long-standing basics of early childhood education: block play, sand/water play, science experiments, cooking, dramatic play, physical activity; lots of opportunities for talking, listening to stories, and engaging with books, songs, and poems; and lots of opportunities for negotiating and solving problems with others (National Association for the Education of Young Children & National Association for Early Childhood Specialists in State Departments of Education, 2003). It is through activities such as these that children come to understand the world and build a foundation that provides the basis for constructing concepts in language, literacy, math, science, and the arts. The many ways that children use symbols in these active experiences build a foundation for them to comprehend and use the abstract symbols they will need at a later age to successfully engage with print and written numbers (Singer, Golinkoff, & Hirsh-Pasek, 2006).

The context needed for these types of experiences is classrooms that are safe, nurturing, joyful places that offer many opportunities for meaningful, purposeful, relevant activities connected to children's cultures, languages, and developmental needs. These contexts, facilitated by teachers who are knowledgeable about how children learn—both generally and in different discipline areas—ensure that young children are prepared for later learning. Subsequent chapters of this book detail how this can be done.

Organizing the Classroom as a Learning Environment

Tell me, I forget.
Show me, I remember.
Involve me, I understand.

—Ancient Chinese proverb

Because research informs us that experience is the trigger that enables children to organize their brains to support the challenges they meet, and because we know that these experiences support the development of the whole child—social, emotional, cultural, linguistic, physical, *and* cognitive—a positive learning environment for young children needs to provide activities to support all of these aspects of growth (Brown & Campione, 1996). To do this, the environment needs to include activity centers that offer opportunities for both hands-on, play-based learning and developmentally appropriate instruction of academic skills. A rich array of materials needs to be available in areas/centers that invite children to inquire, explore, discover, and engage with one another about ideas. Varied types of activities need to be offered throughout the day and provided in a clear and predictable schedule, supported by routines and carefully planned transitions that result in a smooth and well-managed flow of the day.

While these characteristics of an environment for high-quality early learning are necessities throughout the early childhood years, variation in emphases on the different areas should depend on the age/developmental level of the class. Specific examples will be noted in the following discussions.

THE PHYSICAL ENVIRONMENT SUPPORTS ACTIVE LEARNING

The physical arrangement of the classroom should be guided by the foundational goals and purposes of early learning that will prepare children for a changing world: to support them in developing the skills of thinking, reasoning, problem solving, decisionmaking, applying understandings to new contexts, and expressing ideas and sharing them with others. An environment that promotes 21st-century learning goals is not a classroom where knowledge is transmitted by the teacher to passive recipients, often seated in rows of desks, who use materials (the most common being book, pencil, and paper) that are stored in closed drawers or on high shelves where the teacher can control their use. Rather, an environment that promotes young children's development of 21st-century learning goals is arranged into different interest areas or centers that provide opportunities for learning in all of the disciplines—literacy, mathematics, the sciences, and the arts. The teacher is not the focal point of the room or the learning. A wide variety of materials are available and accessible to all children. In this kind of an environment children can test and express their ideas, make decisions, solve problems, apply their own reasoning to diverse situations, and share their learning experiences with others.

The classroom areas/centers need to be clearly defined, each housing a variety of materials for children to use as tools for the disciplinary and cross-disciplinary learning that takes place there. Tables and chairs and/or spaces for individual and small-group work should be available in each area. One large area should be designated as a space for the whole class to gather for meetings. Display spaces for children's work, at their eye level, and storage space for the children's belongings are also staples of classrooms that support high-quality learning for young children.

Activity Areas and Materials Support Disciplinary and Cross-Disciplinary Learning

The following are some of the basic activity centers/areas of a high-quality early learning environment that fosters children's abilities to construct knowledge and understandings:

Figure 2.1. Block Center

A block area that houses a full set of wooden unit blocks, arranged by size and shape, as well as accessories (such as signs, figures, and writing utensils) in low open shelving that clearly demarcates where each block should be stored.

Figure 2.2. Math/Manipulative Center

A math/manipulative area that offers a variety of materials including puzzles, small blocks, Legos, games, tiles, geoboards, attribute blocks, and other hands-on materials that foster children's thinking and problem-solving skills and support the development of the big ideas of math that are appropriate for young children (counting and cardinality, operations and algebraic thinking, number and number sense, measurement and data, and geometry).

Figure 2.3. Library Center

A library area that contains a variety of books arranged by areas of interest and difficulty level—all of which should span the full range of readers who live in the classroom.

Figure 2.4. Writing Center

A writing/drawing area that provides different types of paper, writing/drawing materials (crayons, markers, pencils), stamps, stencils, alphabet charts, and so on, and that can be combined with art materials (for younger children) or separated into its own area as children become more advanced on the literacy development continuum.

Figure 2.5. Art Center

An art area that offers different types of paper and drawing materials (crayons, markers, etc.), as well as paste or glue, scissors, stamps, watercolors, pastels, and tempera paints and brushes, an easel or table available for large painting, collage and construction materials, and other assorted materials such as playdough and clay.

Figure 2.6. Science Center

A science area that includes magnifying glass(es), a sand/water table, animals (guinea pigs, snails, mealworms, etc.), and other items from the natural world (such as plants, rocks, shells, leaves, etc.), depending on the time of the year, curriculum topic, or interests of the children in the classroom. Within this area, children should be given time to experiment with measuring, counting, pouring, and making predictions.

Figure 2.7. Dramatic Play Center

A dramatic play area for younger children (at least through kindergarten) that can be used as a "house" or set up to relive and reflect the ideas and understandings of the particular curriculum focus of the class (i.e., post office, train station, doctor's office, etc.).

Figure 2.8. Media Center

A media center that provides access to computers, audio equipment, a smartboard, and other technology.

Figure 2.9. Cooking Center

A cooking area that contains the tools necessary for preparing snacks or other foods related to the curriculum.

Figure 2.10. Meeting Area

A large meeting area big enough to accommodate the whole class gathering together for group discussions, lessons, stories, and music/movement activities. Generally, the meeting area is in the same place as one of the other larger areas of the classroom—such as the block area or the library—that serves a dual purpose.

Figure 2.11. Outdoor Area

An outdoor play area—if possible, connected directly to the classroom—where children can run, jump, climb, play with wheel toys, grow a garden, and engage in other physical activities.

These activity centers will often include materials that promote many different kinds of learning. The purposes that they serve overlap, nurturing learning in a variety of disciplines. For example, language and literacy are supported everywhere and throughout the day, but especially in the block area (through talking, writing signs, etc.), the writing center, the dramatic play area, the library, and the media center. Social studies are especially supported in the areas for blocks, library, cooking, dramatic play, and science. Math development is featured in the centers involving blocks, construction, woodworking, science, manipulatives, and math. Learning in the arts takes place in the art area, the dramatic play area, and the space for music/movement. Science is supported in the areas designated for blocks, cooking, dramatic play, math, plants, and animals.

Some of these areas are or can be subdivisions of another area—such as a separate table just for playdough, an area just for construction (of recyclable materials such as cartons, cereal boxes, paper towel and toilet paper rolls, etc.), an area for sewing, and so on. And sometimes these areas will be emphasized more in one grade or developmental level over another. The degree to which sole disciplinary instruction is provided in relation to play-based and hands-on learning activities changes as children change and grow and the content and skills appropriate for them to learn become increasingly complex. So, for example, a dramatic play area is critical in the earliest of years when children construct their understandings of the world through role-play and action rather than through the reading, writing, and talking skills they develop in the primary grades. We must remember, however, that regardless of age and developmental stage, all learners need meaningful, purposeful contexts to help them make sense of new knowledge and to learn needed skills.

Arrangement of Activity Centers

When deciding on the location of each area in the classroom, consider keeping activities that are related or complementary and that have similar noise levels and equipment needs near each other. For example, areas that require access to water (such as art and science) should be near each other (and near a sink). Areas that are noisier and complementary (i.e., blocks and dramatic play area) should be adjacent. Quiet areas such as library, media, and writing should be close. Traffic patterns within the classroom should also be considered when arranging centers so that children engaged in related work have materials nearby to support them (i.e., construction area near the art area, or writing area near the library, etc.) or so that quiet areas are not interrupted by the flow of traffic.

Making a drawing or map of your classroom can aid in your planning. Each area should be defined by boundaries that separate them from the other areas. The boundary markers can be low storage shelves, bulletin boards, or even tables and chairs. These boundaries should mark the location of an area in the classroom's organizational scheme without inhibiting children's activity.

Figure 2.12. Classroom Map

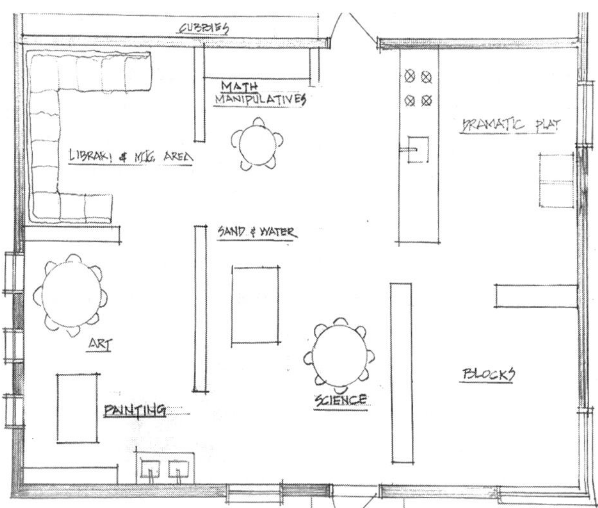

Storing Materials to Support Children's Autonomy

To promote children's independence, autonomy, and sense of self-efficacy, materials housed in the centers should be accessible for children so that they can get what they need on their own. This means that shelving should be open and reachable by small hands. Labels (in the languages spoken by the children) should be posted at each spot where the materials belong, giving children a guide for where to find and return the materials while promoting their literacy development (seeing the written words for the things they need).

Changing Materials to Support Interest and Active Learning

Because we know that interest is a motivator for learning and that active experiences are an important way that young children learn, it is important that classroom centers/areas be provisioned with materials that hold children's interest, are multifaceted, and are developmentally appropriate. No matter how well-organized, stocked, and labeled an area is, it may not hold the interest of the children and will be less educative if the materials are not appropriate to their level of development, if the materials are not meaningful, if they do not allow for active involvement, or if the children have either been overexposed or not exposed enough to the materials prior to placing them in the center. For example, because we know that children construct understandings through experience, a math area that contains only worksheets will be less educative and will be used less than a math area that offers objects with which children can experiment and manipulate (teddy bear counters, stirrers for bundling when learning base, etc.). A dramatic play area transformed into a grocery store that contains only pictures of food will not be nearly as interesting (or rich in learning) as one stocked with realistic food objects and food containers. Active involvement is key to maintaining interest. If materials have the capacity for only one thing to be done with them, only one thing will be done, and then the children will move on. However, children will return to an area again and again when it contains materials that can be used in a variety of ways and at different levels of complexity. The block area is a great example of this. It can be used by 2- and 3-year-olds and it can be used by 7- and 8-year-olds. The youngest children will make simple constructions that lie on the floor; the older children will build complex constructions accessorized with homemade signs and other materials.

Regularly changing the materials in an area also helps to maintain children's interest and involvement. There are several aspects to this point: limited materials should be placed in the areas at the beginning of the school year, with a gradual introduction of more and more complex materials throughout the year. Children first need to be acclimated to how to handle materials before they can sort through and use them productively. As the curriculum and children's skills evolve and the interests of the children evolve, materials can be introduced into different areas that reflect the topics of study. For example, the science area can be focused on planting different kinds of seeds during a plant study, while during a study of rocks and minerals artifacts related to this theme can be introduced. Or, the dramatic play area can be a home, a train station, or a doctor's office depending on the focus of the curriculum.

Print-Rich Environment

Meaningful text should be displayed throughout the classroom in charts that chronicle the learning life of the group. Rather than "decorating" the classrooms with store-bought items, children's original work (their drawings, writing with their own invented or phonetic spelling, their dictated stories) should be displayed throughout the classroom. Charts that chronicle the discussions and learning of the classroom—recipes, documented conversations, curriculum webs, KWL charts (what we *know*, what we *want* to learn, what we have *learned*), graphs that record votes or ideas on important issues, birthday charts, tooth-loss charts, job charts, choice charts, and so on—should also be displayed around the room. This shows children how much their efforts are valued.

Figure 2.13–2.15. Charts

Culturally Relevant and Responsive Materials

Among the print in the environment and throughout the classroom there should be materials, books, images, and artifacts that reflect the diverse cultures, languages, genders, and family configurations of the children and families represented in the class. Children need teachers who see their diversity as an asset, not a deficit. Charts, labels, songs, and texts that include the heritage languages of the children; photos that reflect positive images of people from diverse racial and cultural backgrounds; references to diverse cultures and communities in studies, books, trips, and special events; and efforts to include contributions from the loved ones of the children in the class create an environment that is culturally sustaining.

Figures 2.16–2.17. Culturally Responsive Materials

THE ROLE OF THE TEACHER: FACILITATOR OF LEARNING

In a classroom that is set up for active learning, the role of the teacher needs to be reframed from "teller of information" to "facilitator of learning." This means that the teacher needs to balance teaching specific skills or conveying information with providing experiences that will enable children to construct their understandings and practice the skills needed to make progress. "Each time one prematurely teaches a child something he could have discovered for himself, that child is kept from inventing it and consequently from understanding it completely" (Piaget, 1970, p. 299).

The teacher should not be the center of activity; rather, the classroom's richly provisioned centers/areas should play a prominent role in the children's learning. To enable this, the teacher needs to carefully plan out the experiences of any study, intentionally place materials relevant to what is being studied in each center, observe children carefully while they are at work, and follow up on questions, issues, misunderstandings, or interests that are noticed during choice time sessions.

For example, for a study of the community, a teacher might begin with a read-aloud and a follow-up conversation at a morning meeting time. Texts about different aspects of the community should be placed in the class library as well as in other areas, such as the block center. Photos, posters, and other related print materials might be displayed on the walls. At different points in the study the dramatic play area can be transformed into a store, a train station, a doctor's office, and so on. Which materials to use in the centers, and when to use them, will depend on what the teacher notices about the children's questions and interests. For example, in a community study in one New York City prekindergarten classroom, the children got very interested in buildings. The teacher brought in photos of iconic New York City buildings and provided other related materials. Each day in the block area the children worked on building models of these buildings. Photos were taken of their completed projects and a book was made to showcase the work of the class.

Skill learning was supported through these various activities: reading, through the various books used as resources for the project; writing, through the making of building signs and the class book; math, through the use of different-sized and -shaped blocks; social studies, through discussion of the city; and even science, through discussions about how the buildings stand up and how they were constructed. The teacher was active in driving the learning, but not by telling—rather, by setting up experiences from which the children would learn and by being present at "teachable moments" to ask or answer questions, point out information, or provide guidance in the use of particular skills.

In these ways, the teacher facilitated learning that was relevant to real-life experiences and reflected the interests and understandings of the class.

Figures 2.18–2.23. Buildings

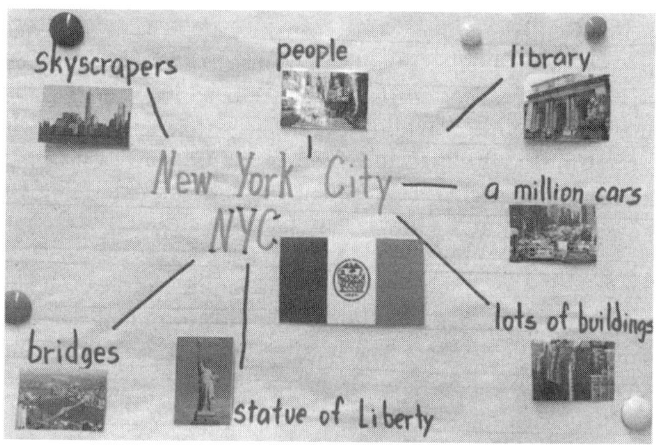

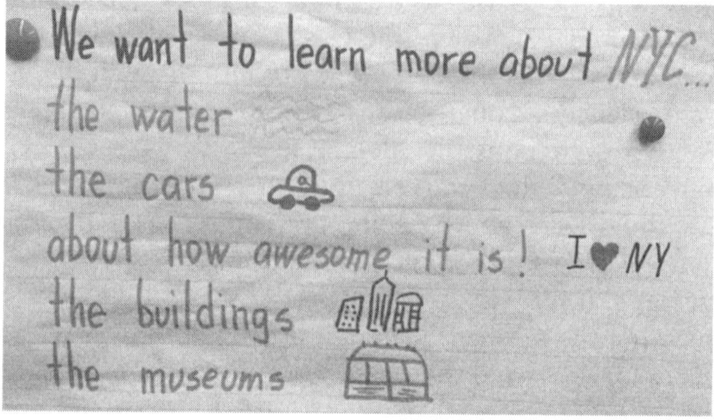

GUGGENHEIM MUSEUM

CHAPTER 3

Routines and Transitions

> The habits we form from childhood make no small difference, but rather they make all the difference.
>
> —Aristotle

As introduced in the preceding chapter, old notions of "teaching as telling," where learning is perceived as receiving information and all children do the same thing at the same time, are being replaced by teaching environments for 21st-century learning, which are based on current understandings of how children learn—that they construct understandings about the world through experience with materials, processes, and relationships. Therefore, the adults charged with supporting children's learning need to plan the day so that this can happen. Teachers need to provide access to different types of activities throughout the day and ensure that opportunities for large-group, small-group, and independent work are offered regularly. They need to guide their support for children by keeping the following principles in mind:

- Learning is a social process, so opportunities for interaction with others in small- and large-group settings should be made available to aid the generation and exchange of ideas. Children should not spend time only in whole-class activities or be forced to sit quietly for long periods of time. Rather, they should have access to a variety of activities throughout the day and spend time working with materials or other children in individual, small-group, and/or whole-group activities at different times during the day.
- Interest is a powerful motivator for learning, so children should be offered choices whenever possible.
- Learners differ in experiences and backgrounds, grow and develop at different paces and in different ways, and have differing strengths and interests, so opportunities for learning need to be provided for those who are more developed as well as for those who need additional help; individualized instruction should support the differentiation of instruction needed to build on and support individuals' varying strengths and needs.

- Powerful learning takes place in meaningful and purposeful contexts, so opportunities should be provided for children to be engaged in projects that encourage them to apply new learning to real-world issues and problems.
- Learning that leads to deep understanding and skill proficiency takes time, so extended periods of time need to be provided for active learning and play-based experiences. Filling out worksheets should not dominate classroom activities.
- Physical activity has been shown to correlate with increased cognitive learning, so children should have an opportunity to play outside every day that weather permits. This should never be sacrificed for more instructional time.
- Language and literacy development are an integral part of all learning, so relevant texts should be available in all centers of the classroom and teachers should read books to children throughout the day, not just at group storytime. Additionally, the classroom environment should be filled with print that narrates the learning taking place in the classroom.

FLOW OF THE DAY

Given these understandings, the flow of an early childhood day in school should include the following: extensive active work time on projects and in centers that provide learning opportunities in all the disciplines; class meetings to discuss and make plans for learning, read and discuss literature, share work, and reflect on learning; work and instruction in all the disciplines in whole groups, small groups, and/or individual settings; outdoor exercise, time for eating (breakfast, lunch, snack), and time for resting (for younger children); trips; other special activities. Children should have opportunities each day to enjoy physical activities indoors and, weather permitting, outside.

Provide a Consistent Schedule

A consistent, flexible schedule offers plenty of time for learning and making choices. It also creates a minimal number of transitions, and limits time in whole groups or seat work. Learning should take place throughout the day in large and small groups and in one-to-one interactions between the teacher and individual children. This helps teachers understand the emerging skills of each child and plan experiences that accommodate each child's own style of learning. A daily schedule should look something like this:

Arrival Activities. Begin the day with choices in various areas of the classroom so that children can be involved and engaged as they transition into school; breakfast may be served at this time.

Morning Meeting. This time should welcome the children and set the tone and plans for the day. Often a read-aloud is conducted, followed by the children selecting centers in which to work during choice time.

Choice Time. Choice time in open-ended center activities of children's choosing should ideally last for at least one hour. The dailiness of this period and the hour-long time devoted to it is to ensure that children can get deeply engaged enough to construct understandings and really follow through on their actions. Chapter 6, "Choice Time in Fanny's Kindergarten Classroom," offers a detailed description of the possibilities that this time holds.

Choice Time Sharing Meeting. Following on the heels of choice time, this meeting is an opportunity to share the learning that has taken place during choice time. As described in Chapter 6, kindergarten teacher Fanny Roman has developed a way to incorporate support for children's writing as part of her choice time sharing meeting. She brings the children together for a meeting after the cleanup of choice time and invites them to think of one thing they did or learned during their choice time. They then sit down at tables or sprawl out on the floor to write and draw about something they did during choice time. Fanny provides them with a special "choice time reflection journal" for this purpose. Entries vary depending on the level of development of children's writing. After about 10–15 minutes, the class reconvenes in the meeting area to share and discuss what they have written in their journals.

Lunch. Meals and snacks are important times for children to replenish, share, and relax together. Whether they bring their own food from home or partake in school-provided food, the lunch—as well as any snack served during the day—is an opportunity to emphasize healthy eating habits and to develop community rituals. Children can be encouraged to take turns setting places at the table and passing out the food, to wait until everyone has been served to eat, to talk to one another while they are eating, and to clean up and recycle. This is a time of the day to build community and consideration for others.

Outdoor Time. Physical activity is essential for children's health and should be a regular part of a daily schedule. Safe and properly supervised physical activity time (preferably outdoors, weather permitting) offers children cognitive, physical, emotional, and social benefits. It should provide free, unstructured play or activity and never be withheld as a punishment. Outdoor time/recess is such an important component of the school day that the American Academy of Pediatrics has a recommendation in its favor (American Academy of Pediatrics, 2013).

Rest. Rest time is required for most programs for younger children. It is a time when they can replenish themselves by sleeping, if needed, or engaging in quiet activities like reading or looking at books.

Afternoon Activities. These should vary depending on the grade: literacy centers; writer's workshop; math workshop; specials such as music, art, science, language supports, trips related to the current study of the class; or more choice time for younger children.

Afternoon Meeting. This is a time for read-aloud and reflections on the day.

Dismissal to Home or Afterschool Activities.

Figure 3.1. Schedule of the Day

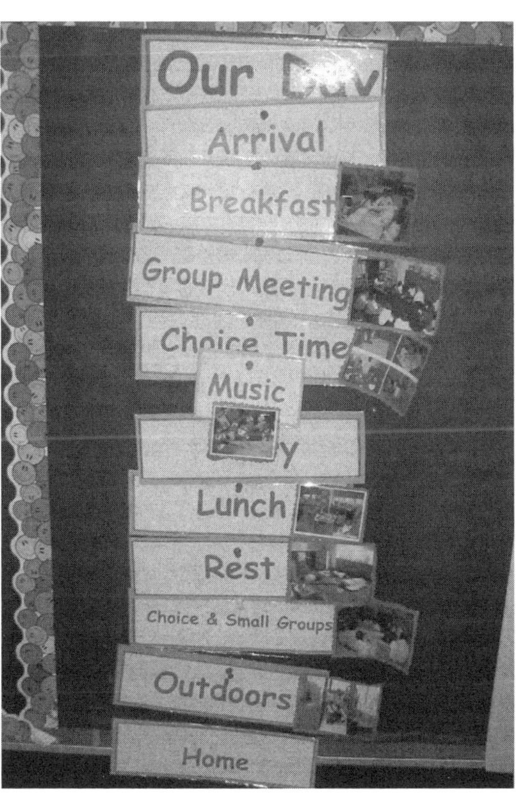

TRANSITIONS

A high-quality early learning environment provides a variety of activities throughout the day. The transitions between these activities—between home and school in the morning and between school and home in the afternoon, from structured activities to cleanup time, from individual and small-group activities to whole-group meetings, going to and from the bathroom or to and from outdoors—all present a challenge for children and for teachers. Transitions present challenges because they signal change and change can be difficult. During transitions, the activities that held children's interests and engagement are suspended, leaving an open space in which stress, anxiety, fears, or homesickness for family can arise. Elisabeth Hirsch (1974) referred to transitions as times that can be "stumbling blocks to education." These stumbling blocks are reflected in the tears shed when little ones say good-bye to their caregivers at the beginning of the school day or year, when a child's kick results in blocks crashing down just at the time a teacher calls "Cleanup," and when arguments or teasing arise as children wait in line to go from one place to another.

For children who are very young and first coming to school, the transition from home to school can be challenging because they are moving away from the familiarity of their home, family, and community to experiencing new environments and new people. These youngest learners need to learn to trust new caregivers or teachers, learn about and understand new contexts, and learn strategies for regulating their feelings and behaviors. The new school environment can ease this transition by being inviting and developmentally appropriate. It can also ease this transition by using the child's familiar caregiver as a point of security. That is why early childhood learning centers serving the youngest of children often require a familiar adult to stay in the classroom during the first days of school to help children acclimate to their new environment. Conquering this first transition to an unknown is an important first step in helping a child to develop self-confidence, adjustment capabilities, and eagerness for new challenges that can last a lifetime.

Other important transitions for young children that deserve attention are when children move from one activity to another in the classroom. In the classroom, transitions are times when children have to cease meaningful and engaging activities such as being involved in a project, a story, or other interesting work. If they don't know what comes next, they might feel anxious, bored, or at loose ends, or start to miss their family, and so on. These feelings can lead to acts of aggression, lack of self-control, regressive behavior, or increased noise.

Teachers also sometimes feel uneasy during transitions. The dread they often experience in calling an end to a productive, orderly, and engaged choice time is because they fear what will happen in the less structured and sometimes hectic cleanup time that follows. How common it is for adults in the room to suddenly feel the urge to leave—to go to the bathroom or make a phone call—when cleanup time approaches! Teachers and children miss the support that meaningful activities provide. It is at this time that anxieties arise about their inability to manage challenging children or about losing control of the classroom. To minimize the anxieties that transitions can unleash, teachers can use a variety of strategies, which are discussed in the following sections.

Establish Regular Routines

It is comforting for children to know what is going to happen to them. Think about your own experiences and the anxiety you feel when going to some place you've never been before. Once you've been there, the next time you go doesn't evoke nearly the same uneasiness. Familiarity can be a real psychic support. To help children prepare for any change, establish clear routines that are followed consistently (with flexibility, of course) every day. These should be discussed and revisited regularly. In addition to the written "schedule of the day" chart displayed prominently in the classroom for all children to see, routines for center time, cleanup, snack, and going home should become well known to all involved. Soon children will be telling each other and/or their family, "First we do ______ , then we do ______."

Provide Advance Warnings

Giving children advance warning about when cleanup or any other transition—such as going home—will take place helps to lessen anxieties caused by change. Think about how you would feel if you were in the midst of reading a great book and someone just pulled it away from you without notice. Rather, if you were told that in 5 minutes you needed to stop reading, you could prepare yourself by strategically aiming to finish a chapter or read to the end of a certain paragraph or page. Children feel the same way about the activities they are involved in. Give them a warning so they can prepare.

Use Songs or Chants to Ease Transitions

A song, chant, or symbol that becomes associated with a transition can help to ease transitions, especially for young children. Stay away from flashing the overhead lights to signal the transition because it can backfire by being overstimulating, especially for children who are sensitive to high sensory input. Rather, a familiar or made-up melody with words that convey information about the transition can help to focus and organize children to prepare for and engage in the coming activities. A welcoming song for group meetings or a good-bye song for the end of the day can do the same.

Clearly Define Tasks

Detailed instructions about what to do and how to do it will help children stay focused and calm. Giving children specific assignments for what area to clean up and how to clean it up will guide them for how to get the job done. Provide additional jobs for children who quickly finish cleaning up their assigned task. Washing tables, using wet sponges from a bucket, is a fun activity that teachers can turn to when children complete a job before others are done; this will help keep children engaged in productive work a bit longer to minimize idle times.

Provide a Clear Future Orientation

If children know what comes next, anxiety will be lessened. So the teachers' job is to help children know what activities are about to happen. If, for example, the transition is cleanup time, directions about where to go and what do next can be helpful in easing anxieties. Often a meeting time will follow cleanup. The children should be directed to go to the meeting area after they have completed their jobs. However, even if the cleanup activities go smoothly, waiting for everyone to gather in the meeting area can be a common additional cause of behavior problems. To avoid the boredom and anxiety of waiting time, teachers need to provide directions for what to do next. Positioning an adult in the meeting area to lead chants, songs, or games can be a helpful strategy to ease the problems that arise from waiting. Or, instructing children to look at or read books (taken from either the library area or a container of "transition books" specifically reserved for this purpose) is another effective strategy.

Minimize Waiting

Waiting causes boredom, which can lead to anxiety and misbehavior. Minimizing waiting throughout the day can help to lessen discipline problems. At the beginning of the day, don't make everyone wait and sit around for the ritual morning meeting. Let work begin as children arrive and then begin the meeting when everyone is there.

Staggering a transition can help to ease the chaos that could erupt from a group making change. If it's cleanup time, the teacher can start with the messiest areas, the ones that take the most time, or the areas in which children have lost interest before calling cleanup for the whole group. The water table, block area, and art area often fit this description. Begin cleaning up with those involved in these areas before calling cleanup for the whole group.

For transitions that involve going to the bathroom or going outside in the winter—transitions that can take extended time—send a few children at a time to get ready instead of making the whole class line up and do the same thing at the same time. Trying to get everyone to do the same thing at the same time rarely works. It often ends up in misbehavior caused by the anxiety that is aroused from waiting.

At story time or when children are lining up, don't wait for absolute quiet from the whole group. A better solution is to start moving or reading the story when a significant number of children are ready. You will find that quiet and cooperation will soon develop as the story or activity begins. Sometimes beginning to read or talk in a soft voice, rather than raising your voice over those who aren't settled, can help to gain attention and focus. Children will quiet down to hear what's being said.

The end of the day is another transition time when waiting can cause anxieties. Children may be struggling with the issue of transferring their loyalties from school to home, they may be fearful of not being picked up or of being left behind, or they may simply be fatigued from holding themselves together throughout the school day. Reducing waiting time by offering the children meaningful, fun, purposeful, relaxing, and cozy activities can help to lessen these kinds of concerns. A special project such as cooking or cuddling together with a great book can be very comforting.

Make the Transition Activity Meaningful and Purposeful

Creating a sense of community and a collective desire and pride about having a nice room can help children to cooperate and be motivated to clean up and handle transitions smoothly. Cleaning up the block area, for instance, can be fun if an adult is present to help find interesting ways to put away the blocks (swooping in to stack them into like-shaped piles when they fall down, handing children "sandwiches" of same-sized pieces and instructing children to find the shape labels that indicate where the blocks should go, or allowing children to invent ways to carry the blocks—piling blocks on a chair and using it as a cart to deliver to shelves). Working in this way will help to establish an involved and satisfying daily life. Performing tasks that are appropriately challenging and feel "just right," supported by trusting and respectful teachers, contributes to a high group morale that will lead to lessened anxiety and fewer difficult behaviors.

Don't Overreact

When children feel anxious, they need more than ever the steady and calm of the adults who are entrusted with their care. Children need to feel safe and protected. They need to know that the adults who are responsible for taking care of them are dependable and are there to protect them. An adult who responds to a child's temper tantrum with an aroused temper of her own will not seem reassuring to the child and will likely heighten the probability of further unacceptable actions. Instead, stay calm, speak softly, and empathize with what you think the child may be feeling. Distinguish between the child's feelings, which you acknowledge, and the child's actions, which you can't allow. Help the child recognize his or her feelings and find solutions that are acceptable and productive. This educative approach will help children move from helplessness toward mastery of their feelings and actions (Erikson, 1963; Jones, 1968). The other children will hear and see how you respond, which will send a message to them all about what will happen to them should any kind of problem arise. If they see that you treat a child, who may be having difficulties, with compassion and in an educative manner, they will be assured that they will be treated similarly should they encounter a similar problem. And this assurance creates a feeling of mutual acceptance and support in the classroom, which helps to lessen the likelihood of difficult behavior erupting.

CHAPTER 4

Understanding the Context in Which You Teach

Because we know that learning is a process that supports connections between learners and new knowledge about the world, it is essential for teachers to know more than just the content they teach. They also need to know how children, in general, learn and develop as well as details about how individual children learn. This involves getting to know each learner, understanding the school and community context in which you teach, knowing about the languages and cultures of the children and their families, and recognizing and utilizing the community's assets and the families' funds of knowledge.

KNOWING ABOUT THE SCHOOL AND COMMUNITY IN WHICH YOU TEACH

Knowing the learner begins with knowing about the context in which the learners live. Before beginning to teach in any school, learn about the school's community. Where do the children who attend this school live? What are the demographics of the neighborhood? What kinds of buildings surround the school—that is, do people live in small homes, apartments, public housing, homeless shelters, or other housing? What services are available? What other facilities—such as parks, stores, health care centers, and restaurants—are available? What cultural institutions are nearby (religious meeting places, museums, public libraries, botanical gardens, zoos)?

Learn about the school as well. What is the school's enrollment—who attends (ages/grades, racial/ethnic/socioeconomic/linguistic backgrounds of the children and families)? What is the environment like—the physical plant and facilities, the atmosphere and tone within the school? How long has the school been in operation? What is the length of the school day and year? How do children arrive to school? Who are the teachers, administrators, and support staff? What is the school's philosophy or mission? What opportunities are there for professional development? What types of programs are offered? What kinds of learning resources are available? What opportunities are there for family/parent involvement?

Knowing about the context and conditions of your school and community will help you to better understand your students, their families, and your colleagues and be responsive to their experiences.

UNDERSTANDING THE CULTURAL CONTEXTS OF YOUR LEARNERS

Critically important to know about and understand are the different cultures and backgrounds of the children in your classroom. What languages are spoken? What countries of origin do the children come from? What cultural and socioeconomic backgrounds are represented? What cultural and religious traditions are observed? What cultural assets or "funds of knowledge" (Moll et al., 1992) do the children and families bring to the classroom? In order to fully understand the perspectives and influences of the children you teach, it is important to familiarize yourself with this information. All the research on development points to the fact that children's languages and cultures matter; that difference can be an asset, not a deficit; and that bilingualism and biculturalism can promote learning (García & Frede, 2010; García & Wei, 2014; García, Lin, & May 2017; Gay, 2013; Ladson-Billings, 1995, 2005; Paris & Alim, 2017).

This research points to the importance of creating classroom environments that incorporate children's cultural and language backgrounds in order to best support their learning. When teachers become knowledgeable about the languages spoken by the children in their class and when they provide ways to connect learning to the languages children speak at home, more effective learning can take place. So while a teacher may not know the home language of every child in the class, becoming familiar with and using key words and concepts, learning about different language patterns and syntax, strategically using translanguaging strategies (multiple languages) to mediate social and cognitive activities (García, Johnson, & Seltzer, 2017), finding people who *do* speak the languages, and seeking out resources in these languages will demonstrate responsiveness to children and families as well as support children's ongoing learning.

Being knowledgeable about and responsive to children's cultures and other aspects of their backgrounds is also a critically important way to support them as they learn. For example, if a child comes from a cultural tradition—like that of many indigenous peoples—that historically has been oriented toward group and shared work, the emphasis on individual presentation and competition that is prevalent in our Western society may clash with their collaboratively oriented ways of interacting. Or, if a child is from a cultural tradition—like that of some African, Mexican, or aboriginal peoples—in which making direct eye contact with an authority figure is considered a sign of disrespect, asking a child to "look at me" while speaking could be disrespectful to that child's culture (Cazden & John, 1971; Hymes,

1967; Philips, 2009; Wax, Wax, & Dumont, 1964; Wolcott, 1967). Being responsive in these ways demonstrates respect for and helps to sustain the cultures of the children's families and communities.

Teaching *about* diversity is as important as teaching *to* diversity (Banks, 2006; Nieto & Bode, 2012). Find out about holidays, foods, traditional clothing, and other traditions and cultural assets of the children you teach so that you can bring these into the classroom through literature, music, photos, and experiences. Make sure the books and photos on the walls in your classroom reflect the diverse cultures and languages of our world and, especially, feature children who look like and speak the languages of the children in your classroom. Make sure to note holidays observed by the families in your classroom, to have snacks that reflect the food preferences of different cultures, and to sing songs and do chants or poems in a variety of languages. A simple "Good morning to you" song can begin the day in the languages spoken by the children in your group.

Attention to these aspects of the setting will impact how the children in your class will learn, and it will support them in culturally relevant ways.

GETTING TO KNOW EACH INDIVIDUAL LEARNER

Having a sense of who your class is culturally is important, but equally important is getting to know the varying strengths, vulnerabilities, interests, and needs of the individuals in your group. An interview with, or questionnaire to, each child's family can provide important information that could be helpful to your teaching. Here is some basic information that might prove helpful to find out:

Home: Where does the child live? In what kind of a dwelling—for example, apartment, single family home, homeless shelter, and so on?

Family: Who is the child's family and what are the relationships among them? Are there siblings? Other extended family members? Other families sharing the space? Who are the child's primary caregivers? Is the child in foster care?

Family work situation: What kind of work do the adults in the household do? Do they work during the day? At night? On weekends?

Home routines: What is life like in the child's home? What time does the child go to sleep? How much screen time do they have? Do they eat together as a family? What do they do on weekends? Do they have access to books or a library? What kind of discipline practices are used in the home?

Family knowledge about the child: What can the child's primary caregivers tell you about the kind of learner the child is? What can they tell you about the child's learning milestones—when she or he first walked, talked, and so on? Or (for older children), what skills and knowledge does the child possess? What do the child's caregivers see as the child's strengths, vulnerabilities, and needs? What are the child's interests? What does the child like to do best in spare time? What are their goals for the child?

Finding out this information about each learner is not meant to be prying. Rather, the purpose is for you, the teacher, to learn from those who know the child best so that you can be attentive to each child's needs.

While learning from a child's family about the home/family/community background is helpful, observing each child in the classroom is also a rich source of information. A teacher needs to listen to and observe children so that she can adapt resources to what she sees and hears from them. She needs to learn about each child's interests so that she can shape the learning in the classroom around them. She needs to be alert to cues and ready to react and respond to the extent that she is able (Cohen, Stern, Balaban, & Gropper, 2015). For example, because young children are transitioning from learning (and expressing their learning) through concrete experiences rather than through words and symbols, she needs to know the child's degree of dependency on concrete examples rather than words; she needs to understand the child's ability to deal with symbols rather than the real thing. And because young children are also transitioning toward understanding the difference between fantasy and reality, the teacher needs to know the depth and limits of their objectivity in thinking.

Other important elements to observe are the child's physical self, the child's ways of relating to others (both children and adults), and the child's styles or preferred ways of learning—what Gardner calls "intelligences" (Gardner, 1983). And, of course, the teacher needs to observe and understand the social/emotional aspect of each child: Is the child outgoing or shy? Is he a leader or a follower? How does the child express feelings? How does she focus, follow through, regulate her actions?

How do you keep track of these individual differences in each child? Through such formats as teacher-kept observations, student-kept records, and actual samples of student work, teachers can develop a unique portrait of each child's learning. This accumulated information can be helpful in planning appropriate learning experiences and in developing curriculum that is responsive to individual students' needs. Strategies for how to engage in this kind of inquiry will be explored in a later chapter of this book.

Part II

LEARNING, CURRICULUM, AND ASSESSMENT

CHAPTER 5

Connecting Play, Purposes, Standards, and Goals

> Each moment we live never was before and will never be again. And yet what we teach children in school is 2 + 2 = 4 and Paris is the capital of France. What we should be teaching them is what they are. We should be saying: "Do you know what you are? You are a marvel. You are unique. In all the world there is no other child exactly like you. In the millions of years that have passed, there has never been another child exactly like you. You may become a Shakespeare, a Michelangelo, a Beethoven. You have the capacity for anything. Yes, you are a marvel."
>
> —Pablo Casals

Understandings about how young children learn, about how to provision classroom environments and structure schedules to support their learning, and about how to connect learning experiences with the authentic contexts of children's lives should provide teachers with a firm grounding in how to create appropriate and supportive curricula. However, another important element that needs to be considered in the development of curricula is the purpose that guides what we do.

THINKING ABOUT PURPOSES AND GOALS

Attention to the purposes of our work helps to ensure that what we do remains true to these goals. Vito Perrone (1991) urges us to keep "large purposes" in mind—to consider what are our aims for education. If we hold to the goal of developing learners who can help steward our changing, challenging, complex world—those who can inquire, weigh evidence, consider others' perspectives, develop deep understandings, apply knowledge and skills to real-world issues, think creatively, pose and solve complex problems, and find joy in the process of learning—then we need to make sure that the classroom activities we design and/or use embody and lead toward those aims.

THE IMPORTANCE OF PLAY AND ACTIVE EXPERIENCES

Long ago, Friedrich Froebel, known as the father of early childhood education, wrote: "Play at this time [in early childhood] is not trivial, it is highly serious and of deep significance. . . . The spontaneous play of the child discloses the future inner life of the man" (1826/2005).

Child development research and theory are in consensus that active, play-based experiences are an optimal strategy to nurture young children to realize those purposes. To do this well, teachers need to take their cue from children's interests and plan opportunities for active play-based learning that fosters children's inquiry, curiosity, motivation, and general socialization. Play is an important way to get to these goals. Many of the skills and characteristics deemed important for children are advanced through play. It is an "important vehicle for developing self-regulation as well as for promoting language, cognition, and social competence" (Copple & Bredekamp, 2009, p. 14). Research has also found that there are links between play and foundational capacities such as memory, self-regulation, oral language abilities, social skills, and success in school (Copple & Bredekamp, 2009). Play is a natural and powerful way to support children's learning and development. Through it, young children can develop the skills and knowledge addressed in early learning guidelines.

PLAY, STANDARDS, AND INTENTIONAL TEACHING

Some argue that play is at odds with learning guidelines and standards. They say that the very existence of early learning standards makes it impossible to run a play-based, developmentally appropriate classroom. This book offers a different perspective: Incorporating guidelines/standards into an early childhood classroom does not mean that the importance of play needs to be diminished. Following early learning guidelines does not necessarily mean a move away from play to didactic teaching. The reason for this is that standards and guidelines are not intended to be pedagogy. They are intended to be a *guide* to *goals* for *what* should be taught, not a *prescription* for *how* things should be learned. "Early learning guidelines address the 'what' that teachers and providers seek to support within children's early development; play deals with pedagogy or how we guide children's development . . . ." (Kagan, Scott-Little, & Frelow, 2009, p. 22).

A play-based strategy for learning is in line with how children learn. Thus, it can be an effective way to foster the external expectations/standards/guidelines developed by the community (the district, state, or national professional associations) for what learners should know and be able to do. Important to remember, however, is that in order to do this, the standards and goals for learning need to be realistic and reachable. This, perhaps, is the issue that leads to a rejection of standards. Some of the standards for early learning, as they have been articulated in some states and some districts, expect from children too much too soon and do not provide for the variations in pace and ways of learning that we know are common in young children's development. Standards and goals need to be carefully reviewed to ensure that they are in line with understandings about how young children learn.

Given developmentally appropriate goals and standards for young children's learning, a meaningful way to work toward supporting them is through a curriculum that integrates the disciplines, builds on what children know and are able to do, and allows children to engage with disciplinary knowledge in meaningful and purposeful contexts at their own unique point on the developmental continuum. For example, when children build with blocks they develop an increasing sense of shape and size and enhanced understandings of weight and balance. When they make signs in the block and dramatic play areas, draw or write at the art table, and document observations at the science table, they gain skills in reading and writing. When they exchange ideas, ask questions, negotiate problems, take turns, and work together in classroom centers, they make gains in their language as well as their social and emotional development. Side by side, children at different developmental levels can work and learn together and make progress on the goals of many standards.

Play-based learning that progresses at each individual's own pace can be used to facilitate the learning of professionally articulated goals/standards/guidelines. Teachers can do this by shifting their thinking and actions—from seeing play-based environments as only "laissez faire" endeavors to seeing some play-based experiences as opportunities for exposing children to the skills and knowledge articulated in early learning guidelines. This intentional infusion of skill building into play calls for a reframing of the role of the teacher—to facilitate activities and interactions that not only support the important social and emotional benefits of play, but that also help children gain mastery of needed skills and construct their own understandings about key concepts.

In the context of this perspective on play, three approaches to teaching are needed to ensure and enhance young children's optimal learning: learning through child-driven exploration in classroom learning centers, learning through explicit instruction, and learning through curriculum studies. The first two of these three approaches are discussed in the rest of this chapter. Learning through curriculum studies is discussed in a subsequent chapter.

Learning Through Child-Driven Explorations in Classroom Centers

As mentioned previously, a most powerful way to support children's learning is through child-driven explorations that take place in centers set up in early childhood classrooms. These explorations take place during choice time provided in these areas and through interdisciplinary thematic extended studies that can be woven throughout the day. The experiences and projects that take place in these contexts can provide for all areas of a child's development (physical, social, linguistic, aesthetic, and cognitive) and incorporate all subject areas. They can provide opportunities for children to make meaningful connections and apply what they are learning to real-world situations while they promote understandings and a strong desire to learn. To utilize these areas in the most optimal way, teachers need to be clear about the skill and knowledge possibilities inherent in the areas and then be intentional about helping children utilize the full range of learning the areas can provide. Below is a discussion of the disciplinary kinds of learning that can take place within different centers.

Block Area. In the block area children are moving about physically and developing dexterity as they balance blocks on one another and experiment with balance and stability. They are developing cognitively as they relate their disciplinary understandings to their buildings. For example, math and science understandings are enhanced as they classify blocks according to size and shape, become familiar with geometric shapes, and enrich their buildings; social studies understandings are enhanced by reenacting and/or creating structures related to the current topic of study; language and literacy skills are practiced as children discuss their ideas with one another and make signs to go along with their created structures; and children's social/emotional development is supported in this area as they collaborate and negotiate with one another when proposing and revising plans for their buildings.

Similarly, other areas of the classroom support children's development in multiple areas.

Dramatic Play. Through dramatic play children are learning social and emotional skills and working out their understandings of knowledge and information they have encountered. As they play, they synthesize past experiences and demonstrate their understanding of acceptable social relationships, revealing their interests and confusions. When they improvise roles and situations, they are engaged in the cognitive thinking that supports learning to read, write stories, and understand the complexities of mathematics.

Art Center. In the art center (to which there may also be attached a playdough/clay center) children have opportunities to express their feelings, ideas, and understandings in a risk-free environment and experiment with many artistic techniques through a variety of materials. As the children cut, paint, draw, and sculpt with the materials stocked in the art center, they get practice with many skills: using scissors and staplers; gluing and taping; learning different ways to fold and tear different kinds of paper; drawing and writing with crayons, pencils, markers, and pens; using hole punchers; painting with different kinds of brushes using watercolors, tempera, acrylic, and finger paints; and constructing sculptures with found materials, clay, wood scraps, and other collage materials. The art center can support the development of children's creativity, confidence, problem solving, perseverance, nonverbal communication, focus, feelings of self-esteem, and abilities to receive constructive feedback and to collaborate.

Writing Center. The writing center is closely related to the art area, especially in the youngest grades. This is because children's first gestures in print are usually drawing. As their abilities to express their ideas connect to symbolic print, marks, and letters, words and sentences begin to appear in children's drawings. Materials that support children to express their ideas and connect them to the symbolic form of letters and words—such as writing utensils (pencils, crayons, markers, pens), different kinds of papers and pads and journals, stamp pads and stamps, and so on—should be strategically placed in this center.

Science Center. At the science center, in which there may be a water/sand table, children have opportunities to experiment, investigate, observe, and question the world around them. It should be stocked with a range of materials such as sorting trays, magnifying glasses, funnels, measuring cups and spoons, containers of different sizes, eye droppers, scales, thermometers, and materials for documentation (clipboards, journals, pens and markers). On display for observation and interaction can be a variety of natural materials that vary depending on the time of year, the interests and topics that arise, and the trips and experiences of the children. These materials might include leaves, acorns, seed pods, pumpkins and gourds; shells and rocks; animals such as snails, worms, bugs, and guinea pigs; or inanimate objects such as gears and other small machines. Through the exploration and experimentation with these materials children get concrete experience with observing and recording data; understanding volume, weight, and size; and learning about how things work. They engage in the practices articulated in the national science standards (Next Generation Science Standards, 2016): asking questions and defining problems; planning and carrying out investigations; analyzing and interpreting data; using mathematical and computational thinking; constructing explanations and designing solutions; engaging in argument from evidence; and obtaining, evaluating, and communicating information.

Cooking Area. A cooking area is an extension of the science area in which children learn about scientific concepts (what happens when a liquid is heated—it turns to a gas; when solid materials are mixed with water or oil—they dissolve; etc.). Recipes for what is being cooked offer opportunities for reading and writing and provide concrete experiences with mathematical concepts (measuring, fractions, weight, volume, etc.)

Math/Manipulatives Center. In the math/manipulatives center children can have opportunities to play with materials that help them develop a sense of agency and self-confidence in math (Clements & Sarama, 2011). They can use materials to develop basic concepts of counting, data analysis, measurement, number operations, number sense, shape, pattern, sets, and spatial relationships, and they can develop mathematical reasoning (Early Math Collaborative, Erikson Institute, 2014). Materials such as pattern blocks, attribute blocks, geoboards, clocks and timers, puzzles, games, straws, and connectors can help children to explore, practice, and consolidate their understandings of these concepts.

Library Area. A library area in the classroom that children can use independently is a vital component of every early childhood classroom. In prekindergarten or kindergarten, a classroom library should be a place where students can go to look at or "read" books, intentionally selected for an easily accessible display shelf, that relate to the current class theme or study (be it a study of animals, a study of a particular author, etc.). As children move up in the grades, the classroom library area should also contain bins of books organized and color-coded by difficulty level as well as labeled bins that sort books into categories and topics of interest. Often built around a meeting area where the whole class gathers for group meetings, the library area should also be a place where children can sit and read. Here children can seek out a wide range of informational texts, stories, and poems. As they explore different texts they build their technical skills, they learn that text provides valuable information, and they can develop a love of reading.

Throughout all of the experiences in the varied centers of an active learning classroom, development of disciplinary content knowledge and skills are taking place. The meaningful and purposeful contexts of the experiences in these areas offer rich opportunities for young children to be exposed to, learn about, and have opportunities to practice important knowledge and skills.

Learning Through Explicit Instruction

Explicit instructional times in a classroom for young children can also play an important role in supporting their learning. The frequency of these times increases as children move up in the grades. But all children can benefit from group meetings where teachers read a book, lead a discussion, or introduce children to carefully planned topics, skills, or information. Examples include introducing children to the work of an author or teaching a mini-lesson on punctuation (what is a period, an exclamation mark, or a question mark).

Guidance and facilitation related to skill learning can also take place during times designated for instruction in the content of the disciplines—literacy blocks (more on that in a later chapter), math workshops, or times set aside in the schedule for experiences that focus explicitly on science, social studies, or other disciplines.

Intentional guidance by a teacher can be given as she or he moves around the classroom to support individual children during center or choice time. For example, attention to skills might happen while helping a child with a strategy during a game or assisting a child who is writing a sign in the block area. Lots of opportunities for such explicit instruction are also possible during activities set aside for independent work on reading and writing, such as times for journal writing or literacy centers. Here is when a teacher can help a child sound out a word or guide her to locate a word from the environmental print (class list, word wall, or other charts) in the room as she is writing and drawing in a journal, updating a list of texts read, or making a card to a friend or family member. This is true for other disciplines as well: teachers can help children deepen their math knowledge by drawing attention to different shapes and sizes of blocks in the block area or by asking explicit questions related to scientific understandings about the changes in substances when mixing solids and liquids or baking bread. Key to enhancing the learning in these instances are the comments and questions posed by the teacher. These comments and questions need to take advantage of teachable moments and stimulate the learner to take a closer look, think about why, and discover a path toward an answer.

The following chapter offers examples of how a teacher balances child-directed work in centers, facilitates whole-class inquiries, and nurtures skill and knowledge development in these active learning experiences.

CHAPTER 6

Choice Time in Fanny's Kindergarten Classroom

Nurturing Learning Through Inquiry and Play

This chapter offers images of how child-directed active learning in classroom centers and whole-class inquiries based on children's interests nurture skill and knowledge development in a kindergarten classroom. It shares the work of Fanny Roman, a kindergarten teacher at P.S. 244Q—The Active Learning School, a public elementary school in Flushing, Queens, in New York City. Video images of Fanny's classroom can be found at highqualityearlylearning.org/kindergarten-videos-2/.

DAILY CHOICE TIME PROVIDES OPPORTUNITIES FOR ACTIVE LEARNING AND INQUIRY

A daily choice time in richly provisioned centers or areas provides a variety of open-ended experiential opportunities for children in Fanny Roman's kindergarten class to make choices and have a voice in decisions about what and how they learn. One hour each morning is dedicated to this time. Based on understandings that choice motivates learning (Brophy, 2013; Cordova & Lepper, 1996; Stipek, 2002), Fanny gives children the opportunity to choose a center in which to work. Options include areas for block play, dramatic play, art and construction, sand/water investigations, writing, table games that focus on mathematics and reading, and an area for those who are helping to accessorize the block area.

Morning Meeting

A morning meeting of the whole class begins the day. There, children share information about themselves and their families, ideas and wonderings about topics to study, and questions about their understandings of the skills and information they are learning. The meeting concludes with them selecting where they want to work during choice time; those who choose blocks on Monday morning commit to a week-long project in that center. The block builders begin their week by planning together what they will build, first drawing their ideas on a whiteboard that is stationed in a corner of the center.

Figure 6.1. Block Builders

The children work on their constructions every day, and leave them up for the entire week. Other children select to work in a block accessory area, where they assist the builders by adding drawings, signs, and/or constructions to the block constructions. For example, while one builder's group drew and built an airport (which is near the school), some of their classmates worked in the block accessory center to make vehicles, signs, and airline tickets. Another time, while a builder's group drew and built the local library, some of their classmates made books and bookshelves out of paper and cardboard.

The Aviation Study

During the winter months of the school year, an inquiry on aviation took place in the classroom. It was an outgrowth of a bird study that was launched earlier in the fall as a result of a child bringing a book about flamingos into school. After a read-aloud of the book to the class, children had lots of questions, such as "Do flamingos fly?" and "What makes a bird a bird?" Taking her cue from this interest of the children, Fanny brought lots of books and Internet resources about birds into the classroom. Children explored these resources, reflecting on what they learned in their conversations, in their writings—both fact and fiction—in their drawings, and in their art constructions (papier-mâché birds). After weeks of this kind of investigation, a class conversation about what makes a bird fly led to the children wondering about other things that fly.

Figure 6.2. Wondering Chart

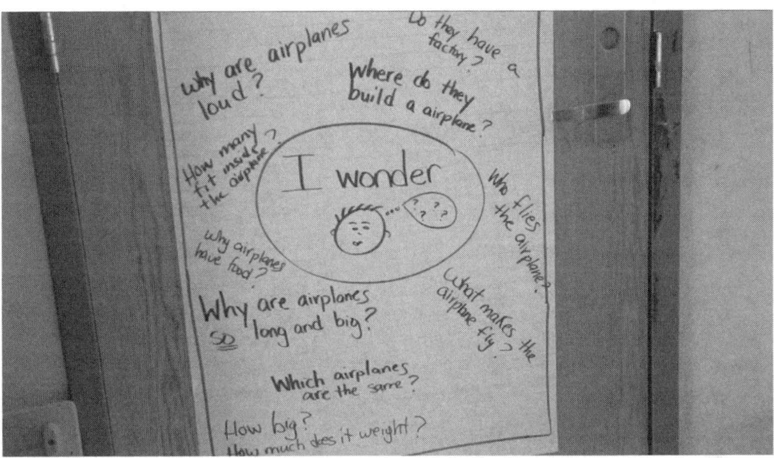

Thus, the aviation study was born. It involved readings about planes and airports, creating drawings and three-dimensional constructions of airplanes, transforming the dramatic play area into an airport, the aforementioned block-area construction of an airport, outside walks to observe planes in the sky, and a trip to the nearby airport.

Figure 6.3. Aviation Books

Figure 6.4. Airport Play

Weaving School-Based Standards and Skills into the Curriculum

Fanny used the children's questions, interests, and developing knowledge to provide active learning experiences, connected to these real-world contexts, to nurture disciplinary skills and knowledge (writing, math, reading, social studies, science).

Figure 6.5. Author Study Chart

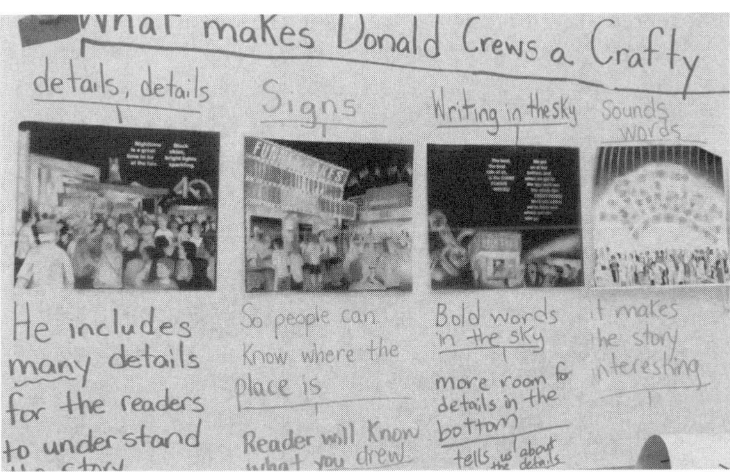

In the process, she also learned about her students—their areas of strength and those needing attention. In the midst of this investigation she introduced a "choice-time journal reflection" into class routines. This took place at the conclusion of choice time, after cleanup, and involved the children sitting at tables to write and/or draw in special journal books about what they did or learned during the day's choice-time activity.

Figure 6.6. Choice-Time Journal Writing

The journal reflection lasted for about 10 minutes and was followed by a whole-class sharing meeting in which the teacher selected a few children each day, representing varying places on the continuum of literacy development, to display and explain what they wrote.

Figure 6.7. Choice-Time Journal Share

After each child's presentation, questions, noticings, and wonderings were expressed, concluding with expressions of appreciation for each contributor.

In these ways, through a mix of individual, small-, and whole-group interaction and instruction, Fanny was able to support the children to gain proficiency in the school-based standards, objectives, and skills/knowledge required by the district while also nurturing her students' development of their sense of self-efficacy and critical faculties. As she worked in this way, she demonstrated her trust in children's capacities to learn and in her ability to "join with the learner" (Weber, 1991) to build on and extend her planned curriculum.

BUILDING ON CHILDREN'S REALITIES AND STRENGTHS

Fanny gives conscious attention to the differing experiences, resources, and expertise of the children and families in her classroom. She aims to forge strong connections with children's families, the majority of whom are speakers of languages other than English. Because so many family members work during the day, she communicates with parents and caregivers through a newsletter that explains current units of study. She also invites families to participate in the class's work by asking them to send in resources for the class's learning and/or to attend school meetings in the evenings. For example, one child's mom, who had recently returned from a trip to her home country, sent in boarding-pass tickets for the aviation study. Other family members sent in items to use in class studies that they learned about from the monthly curriculum newsletter. The father of one child, after his son was observed at the playdough table expertly making pretend sushi, revealed that he was a sushi chef and was subsequently invited to visit for the 100th-day-of-school celebration. He brought in 100 pieces of sushi!

A RANGE OF SCHOOL SUPPORTS NURTURE TEACHERS' LEARNING

Fanny credits support from her school for making possible the rich learning that takes place in her classroom. Thanks to the school's principal, several consultants are available to work with the teachers. One offers support for how to integrate play and inquiry work with literacy and other academics. Another offers support for shared and guided reading and other literacy-related activities. And still another consultant focuses on math. Additionally, the principal allots time for the teachers to meet as a grade and in small groups to discuss curriculum. One project the teachers took up during the time of this documentation was examining their units of study for ways to incorporate questions to stimulate more discussion in their mini-lessons.

Perhaps the most important element of support from her school that Fanny acknowledges is simply the fact that she is given permission to allow her students to learn through play. As she stated in an interview, "I am allowed to do all this and still have that integrity of what early childhood is all about with the play. I am still able to fit it all in and have play. . . . That makes such a difference. Such a difference. . . . I feel fortunate that I can fit it into my day and know that it's okay. . . . Not every school has this. . . . They [the children] are excited, so excited to learn. That's what motivates me every day. There is always a wondering question. They are ready every day to learn, and they have so much curiosity that it keeps me going and I don't mind going that extra mile because I just love seeing it happen."

NURTURING 21ST-CENTURY SKILLS THROUGH ACTIVE LEARNING

This description of Fanny's classroom demonstrates how public school kindergarten can provide a culturally relevant and developmentally appropriate learning environment for a diverse population, many of whom are immigrants, emergent bilinguals, and from low-income backgrounds. Rather than taking the all-too-common approach of focusing on prepping children with academic skills so that they can "catch up" with their more resourced peers, this classroom offers images of possibility for how young children's development and learning of the skills and knowledge needed for a changing world can be nurtured through active experiences in classroom centers, responsiveness to diversity, and attention to social–emotional development. This description of Fanny's work adds to our understandings of what high-quality early learning looks like and how it can foster, in a joyful context, the kinds of critical/creative thinking, perspective sharing, and social/emotional competencies needed to sustain a just and equitable democracy.

CHAPTER 7

Learning Through Interdisciplinary Curriculum Studies

> Good teachers possess a capacity for connectedness. They are able to weave a complex web of connections among themselves, their subjects, and their students so that students can learn to weave a world for themselves. The connections made by good teachers are held not in their methods but in their hearts—meaning heart in its ancient sense, as the place where intellect and emotion and spirit and will converge in the human self.
>
> —Parker J. Palmer, *The Courage to Teach* (1998, p. 11)

In addition to learning through center-based activities and explicit instruction in either whole-class or informal settings, a powerful vehicle for moving knowledge and skill development forward is a study or inquiry of a theme or topic undertaken by the whole class.* Whether the curriculum is handed down from the school/district/state, whether it is commercially bought, or whether it is designed by the teacher, an interdisciplinary study offers rich opportunities for content-based learning as well as for using skills and knowledge in real-life settings. Examples of curricula that provide multidisciplinary experiences are studies of the family, of the community, of plants, of animals, and so on. Regardless of the origin of the study, the teacher's job is to ensure that powerful learning takes place by provisioning the classroom to accomplish the following:

- Build on what you know about how children learn: Provide abundant play and active experiences in multiple modalities that nurture questions and inquiry.
- Reference the goals/standards/guidelines of your school, district, and/or state, and intentionally keep track of how these can be and are infused in play-based activities.

*Some of the ideas from this chapter were developed in collaboration with Nancy Gropper and Rima Shore, my writing and thought partners for a document produced for a meeting of early childhood educators called *Joining with the Learner*, held at the City College of New York on June 17, 2016.

- Build on what you know about the particular children whom you teach—what the late Lillian Weber (1991) referred to as "joining with the learner."

JOINING WITH THE LEARNER

"Joining with the learner" is essential to providing a "learner-centered" or "child-centered" classroom. Yet it is an aspect of teaching that is in need of attention in the context of the current wide use in schools and districts of premade commercial or district-mandated curricula. While some of these curricula are designed to take into consideration how children learn (through active, play-based experiences) and are connected with early learning standards and guidelines, it is argued here that an externally developed curriculum can never—on its own—be fully responsive to the unique children who are its recipients. Joining with the learner is what connects experiences that support the development of knowledge and skills expressed in early learning guidelines with the understandings, interests, and needs of the learners. Joining with the learner is what a teacher/caregiver does to ensure that the learning or support offered to children is informed by and responsive to their needs, interests, understandings, and backgrounds. It is realized by close observation of children: what they look at, where their curiosity leads them, how they make sense of what they are learning, and what feelings they express while doing so.

Psychologist Jerome Bruner (1995) described this as "joint attention," a "meeting of the minds" between an adult and a child that helps young learners experience their own agency, and that offers them deeper, more engaging, more nuanced ways of knowing the world and themselves. Neuroscientists call this "serve and return" (National Scientific Council on the Developing Child, 2004)—a reciprocal process of reaching out and responding between children and the adults who care for them, which research confirms is essential to healthy development.

For teachers, joining with the learner means more than just following a script of a required curriculum or even delivering a curriculum they have developed on their own (no matter how well it is designed), but rather making sure that the teaching is informed and shaped by input from their learners. It means meeting learners where they are and guiding them from there to help move them forward. It means creating settings and opportunities where children's exploration can be extended.

Teachers find out how to join with the learner by observing and noticing them, glimpsing the world as they see it, honoring and meeting them where they are, and responding to their feelings and their intentions. In this way, teachers can take what they know about the children they teach to inform and shape future teaching and caregiving. Establishing this approach as an essential practice strengthens support for optimal development. The key to this process is close observation of and connection to those being served. This idea will be further developed later in this book.

DESIGNING YOUR OWN STUDIES VERSUS USING PREDESIGNED CURRICULA

Many schools and districts require the use of predesigned curriculum units. These range from developmentally appropriate and culturally responsive/relevant plans that incorporate current knowledge of how young children learn to make plans and/or scripts based on notions of learning that emphasize teaching as telling, rote memorization, isolated skill development, and inappropriate topics for young children.

Joining with the Learner Within a Predesigned Curriculum

Almost any predesigned curriculum—no matter how "good" it is—can be strengthened by joining with the learner, as discussed previously. The key is to ensure that the children understand what is presented and that it is framed in contexts that reflect their realities. Don't just follow a script. Connect new information with children's experiences, cultures, and communities. Ask questions and examine their work to make sure that they get what has been taught before moving on. Find ways to access their understandings so that ideas and questions can be pursued to support all students to make sense of and incorporate the new knowledge. Wherever possible, provide active learning experiences to aid children's processes of constructing new knowledge.

This process takes time—often longer than provided for in school and district pacing schedules. It requires time and patience for learners to have the chance to figure things out, to "mess about" with materials and ideas (Hawkins, 1965), and to make "mistakes"—an important window for teachers into learners' thinking that offers opportunities to guide and scaffold the next steps for learning. Getting the right answer is not enough. The goal needs to be that educators ensure that learners know why they do what they do and understand the underlying concepts.

The critical point here is that teachers need flexibility to carry out curriculum. So, if you are required to teach a prescribed curriculum, following are some suggestions for how to make sure you are including the children in the work.

First, find out what the children know about the topic to be studied. Making a KWL chart (Figure 7.1) with the class (what we *know*, what we *want* to learn, what we have *learned*) is one effective way to begin.

Figure 7.1. KWL Chart

What we know	What we want to know	What we have learned

This chart can serve as a document of the class's learning, recording the children's prior knowledge and experiences as well as their questions and interests. As the learning progresses, the chart records new knowledge gained and becomes part of the history of the learning of the class. During a discussion at a class meeting, teachers can record what children already know. Even things they say they know that may be incorrect should be recorded so that the misconceptions can be referenced later when the "what we have learned" column is filled out.

Another way to include children in the work is to offer them opportunities for choices wherever possible. For example, if you are required to study animal habitats (as described in Chapter 11 on the Bronx River study), allow the class to select what animals to study and give all children a choice of what particular animal they want to become an expert about.

Before you move on from one prescribed activity to the next, pick up on and pursue the children's questions. For example (again, from Chapter 11's Bronx River study), if you are studying the river and a question arises about how fast the river flows, design a hands-on experience for the children to address this question. One way is to take a trip to the river to actually count how long it takes a leaf to travel from one point on the river to another.

Within the context of the prescribed curriculum, extend activities and/or investigations based on the children's interests. For example, in a study of the community in Emma Markarian's prekindergarten class (described in the chapter to follow), as a result of a walk around the neighborhood the children got interested in the subway station. To be responsive to this interest, Emma created an additional set of learning experiences to explore the subway station more in depth.

Joining with the Learner in the Context of Designing Your Own Curriculum

If you are fortunate enough to be in a setting where you are allowed to design your own curriculum, the guidelines discussed in the previous section also apply. The central theme or focus of the class study can be selected in several ways—based on the requirements of your school/district (a required unit or standard), a question that has come up in the class that you think is worthy of pursuit, or an interest or idea of your own that you believe can offer rich opportunities for learning.

To help you plan, consider the following process: After deciding on the theme, create a KWL chart as described previously, an "I wonder" chart that records all of the children's questions, or a web that documents all subjects that the children think are connected to the topic.

Figure 7.2. What We Know Web

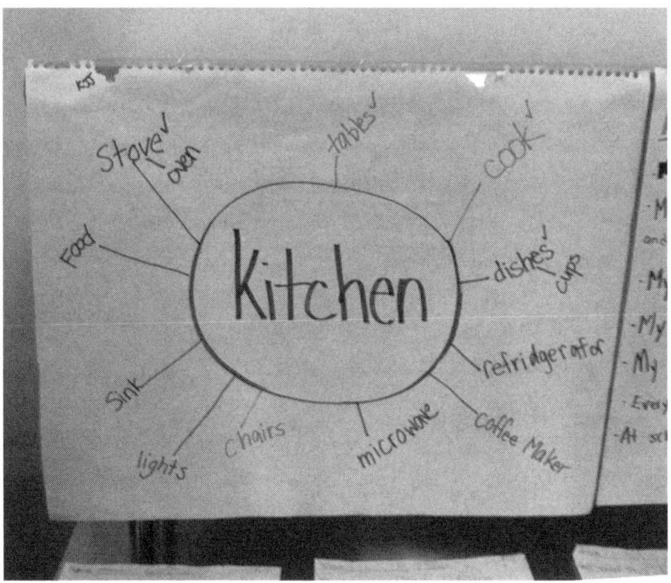

Then, begin planning the set of learning experiences you want to provide for the class. Write down the theme or central focus of your study in a circle in the middle of a page. Draw spokes to all of the different disciplinary content areas, and jot down what in each content area can be addressed or learned through this particular theme.

Then create a table that lists all the different content areas and the experiences you can provide for your class that will expose them to skills and information in the different content areas.

And finally, create another document to show what standards you are addressing in the different content areas and in the different domains (i.e., social, emotional, and physical development.

For one example of how to do this, see Figures 7.3, 7.4, and 7.5, from a study of restaurants that was an extension of a study of the neighborhood/ community in a prekindergarten class.

Figure 7.3. Web for Content Areas Connected to Theme

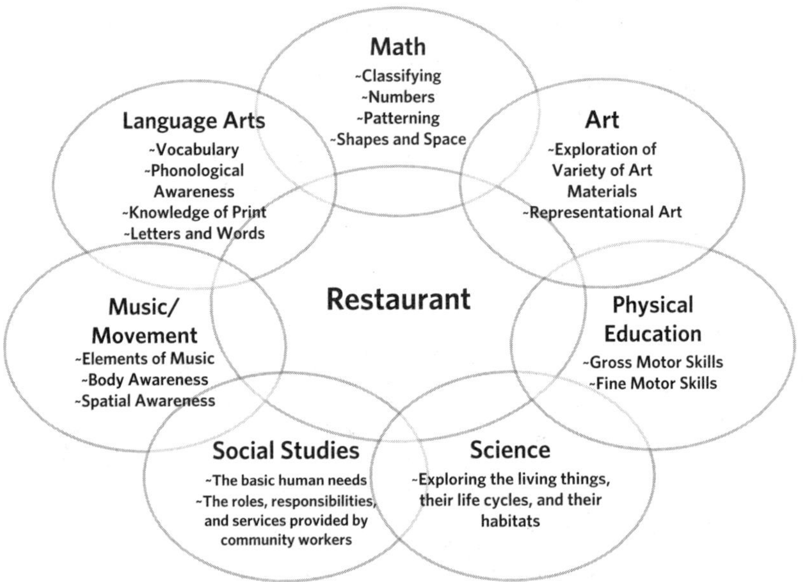

Figure 7.4. Content-Area Experiences

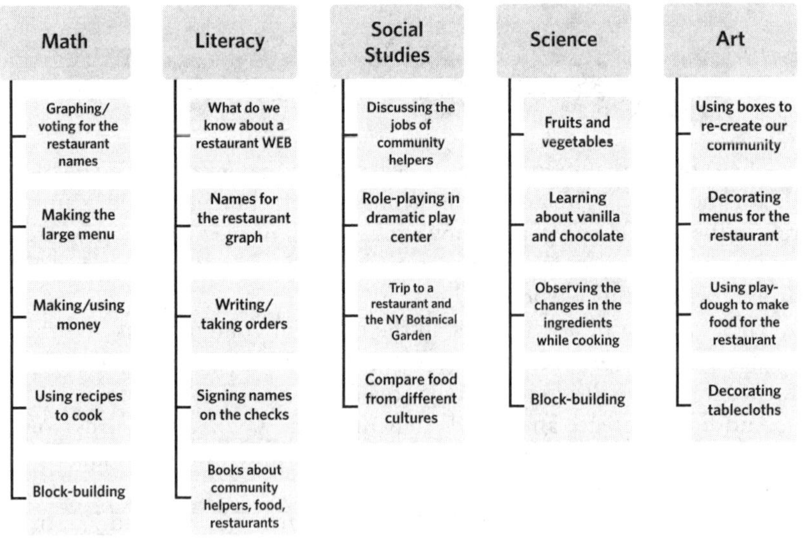

Figure 7.5. Standards

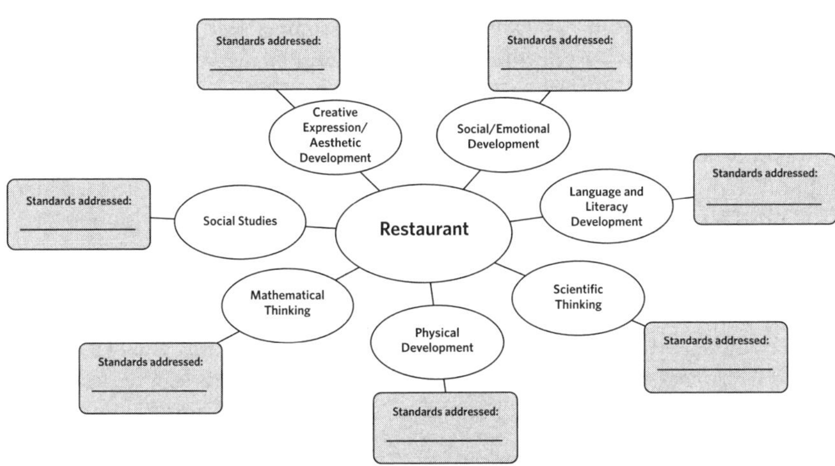

Planning in this way will ensure that you are supporting your learners holistically *and* that you are taking into consideration the standards/expectations/goals held by your school/district/community. In this way, you become an intentional teacher who addresses *all* important aspects of students' learning.

As you consider each experience you want to provide, it could be helpful to create a learning experience plan. This is a useful process that can help you think about what you are doing and why, how it relates to your learners, and how you will know how the experience went. The plan should address the following questions:

- What is the "central focus" (the theme, goals, purpose, or big ideas) of the overall study you are planning?
- What are the district or state standards you will be addressing?
- What are the objectives of each experience in the study that you are planning?
- How does each experience build on the children's prior knowledge and experiences?
- What strategies will you use to ensure that you are supporting all different kinds of learners and their needs?
- What resources and materials will you need for each experience?
- What vocabulary development will you be supporting through these experiences?
- How will you assess what the children in your class are doing so that you can keep track of their progress?

The chart in Figure 7.6 offers a way to keep track of your responses to these questions. The top part is for your overall study, and the bottom part can be reproduced for each learning experience. Taking the time to answer these questions as you draft your plans will ensure that you are being mindful of the unique understandings and experiences of your learners as you progress through a study and support their learning. It is always wise, however, to consider these plans as a draft, subject to modification depending on the questions, interests, paces of learning, and actions of the learners in your class. Only in that way can you stay true to the learning needs of the children.

The following two chapters provide examples of how curriculum studies that join with the learner use some of the tools just described. The first one recounts a study that emerges out of questions raised by the class in the course of a prescribed curriculum. The second depicts a teacher-designed study that flows from the teacher's observations and responsiveness to the interests of the class.

Figure 7.6. Learning Experience Plan Template

<table>
<tr><th colspan="2">FILL OUT BELOW FOR THE ENTIRE STUDY</th></tr>
<tr><td>Central focus (theme, goals, purpose, big ideas) of your study</td><td>Standards addressed in the study</td></tr>
<tr><td colspan="2">Vocabulary of study: What vocabulary will be introduced/developed/supported throughout this learning segment? (At least one of the 3 to 5 experiences should provide opportunities to develop, practice, and/or use targeted vocabulary identified for the segment.)</td></tr>
<tr><th colspan="2">FILL OUT BELOW FOR EACH LEARNING EXPERIENCE IN YOUR STUDY</th></tr>
<tr><td colspan="2">Learning experience plan #____</td></tr>
<tr><th>Component</th><th>Explanation</th></tr>
<tr><td>1. Describe the learning experience: What will you and the children be doing?</td><td></td></tr>
<tr><td>2. What are the learning objectives specific to this experience?</td><td></td></tr>
<tr><td>3. How does this experience build on the children's prior knowledge/experience—in their past learning or in previous learning experiences?</td><td></td></tr>
<tr><td>4. What instructional strategies will you use to be responsive to diverse children's needs? What, if any, supports or accommodations will you need to provide for children with special needs?</td><td></td></tr>
<tr><td>5. What resources and materials will you use?</td><td></td></tr>
<tr><td>6. What assessment will you use to assess children's learning in this experience (i.e., "informal," such as observational notes, audio or video documentation; "formal," such as checklists, work sample with rubric, etc.)?</td><td></td></tr>
</table>

CHAPTER 8

Joining with the Learner Through a Required Curriculum

The Subway Study in Emma's Prekindergarten Classroom

This chapter features an example of teaching from a New York City public school classroom in a high-need community serving young children from diverse cultural and linguistic backgrounds. Even though Emma Markarian, the teacher, was obligated to follow a required curriculum, she figured out how to shape instruction in ways that were responsive to her students and to infuse the skills and knowledge of required standards into meaningful, purposeful experiences.

As part of a larger study of the community, Emma utilized her knowledge that children's interests are a motivator for learning to invite the children to take a vote to determine which aspect of the community they wanted to investigate more deeply.

Figure 8.1. Vote Chart

The subway station was a unanimous choice. The class began their investigation by reading books about trains.

Figure 8.2. Train Books

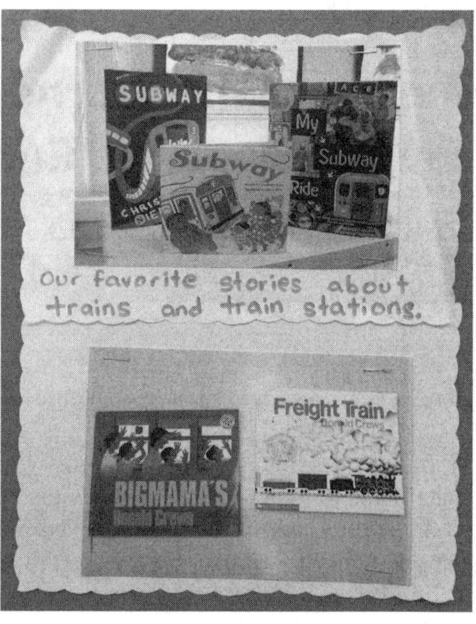

Then they took a walk to the subway station near the school. Upon returning, they made a chart about what they knew about trains.

Figure 8.3. What Do We Know About a Train Station?

At other class meetings they discussed different modes of transportation, making a chart of how they traveled to their grandmother's house.

Figure 8.4. How We Get to Our Grandmother's House

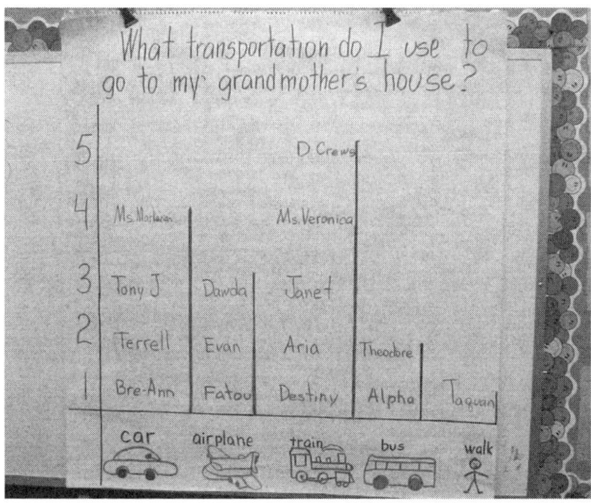

In subsequent days, the class processed their learning—from their readings and the trip—by creating a subway station in the classroom's dramatic play area. The children made their own subway maps and signs for the different trains that traveled through the station.

Figure 8.5. Subway Map

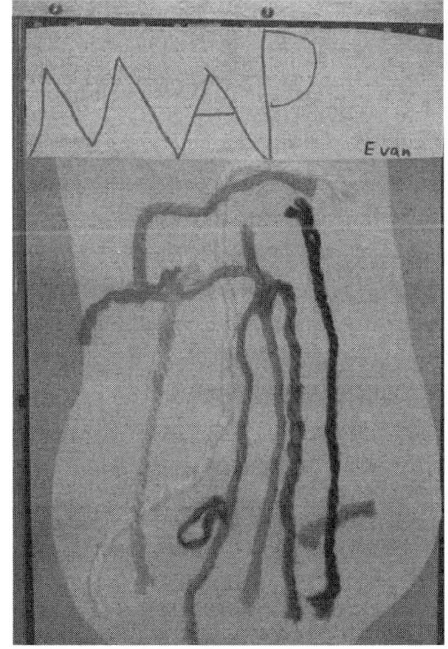

Figure 8.6. Station Signs

They made their own MetroCards, which they bought and sold with pretend money at a ticket booth that they created.

Figure 8.7. Ticket Booth

They drew advertisements for the subway walls and "published" a replica of the free newspaper that is available at actual train stations. The children also demonstrated their learning through the structures they built in the classroom's block area . . .

Figure 8.8. Block-Building

. . . as well as in the writings and drawings they produced in the art and literacy areas and the songs, chants, and poems they recited at class meetings. The finished subway station in the dramatic play area looked like this:

Figure 8.9. Subway Station in the Dramatic Play Area

KEY FEATURES OF JOINING WITH THE LEARNER

Emma was able to craft such an engaging study by digging deep into the cracks and crevices of the required curriculum to shape experiences responsive to her learners. She harnessed children's interests and background knowledge (the subway and their neighborhood) into meaningful and purposeful activities that intentionally introduced new knowledge and skills (guided by the standards) and that offered opportunities for inquiry and critical thinking. Building each activity from her assessment of how children were progressing toward overall goals, she infused literacy skills in the study's readings, conversations, and writing experiences (making subway signs and advertisements, the MetroCards, the newspapers, etc.). Math learning was embedded in the charts that notated election results and in dramatic play with the money used at the subway's ticket booth. Social studies knowledge was developed by exploring and noticing details of the community. And social/emotional development was nurtured as the children listened to and took turns with one another as they worked on projects.

The study's different kinds of activities were intentionally designed to offer opportunities for children with varying strengths and at different stages of development to demonstrate what they knew and could do and to work at their own pace on skill development. So, for example, the child who was just beginning to write was provided with many opportunities to make drawings and phonetic spellings of the study's important vocabulary or to access conventional spelling of these words by consulting class-made charts; the child who was already an independent reader and writer was given opportunities to further her development by reading additional texts on her own or by completing writing assignments designed to extend specific skills.

WHAT IT TAKES TO MAKE THIS KIND OF TEACHING HAPPEN

To teach in the way described here, educators need to be knowledgeable and skillful as well as committed to ensuring that all children learn. They need to deeply understand learning and development and use these understandings to craft learning experiences that build on and *join with* the knowledge children bring to the classroom. As they guide their teaching with standards, they need to remember the larger purposes of education:

> [creating] men and women who are capable of doing new things, not simply repeating what others have done—men and women who are creative, inventive and discoverers . . . who can be critical, can verify, and not accept everything they are offered. (Piaget, in Greene, 1978, p. 80)

Some teachers who do this kind of teaching do it in schools that resonate with these purposes. Others who are not in such settings often find themselves struggling alone, trying to stay true to their values in the face of mandated and/or scripted curricula designed to produce uniform student outcomes in a uniform way. But many teachers realize that required, sometimes scripted curricula (even in the form of integrated themed units of study) cannot substitute for teaching that is tailored to connect with the prior experiences and understandings of the children being taught. So they stretch, bend, elaborate on, and/or work with and around the required curricula to develop meaningful and purposeful, active experiences that build on their students' ideas, interests, and strengths.

This kind of teaching is what is needed to ensure that *all* children get access to high-quality education. To realize this kind of teaching, we need to invest in building teachers' capacities to craft instruction that is responsive to children and their diverse ways of learning. This kind of investment involves providing teachers with opportunities to enrich their thinking and to grow their own skills by sharing with others in professional communities—through grade team meetings, support from coaches, schoolwide study groups, and other such opportunities. When teachers are supported in this way, conditions are set to sustain the capacity for continuous learning throughout the entire educational system.

We know that it is possible to realize this kind of teaching in diverse public school settings. The teaching described here offers proof positive. Now the challenge is to garner the resources and the will to make it happen on a large scale. Doing this is our best hope for preparing *all* the children in our nation's schools to succeed in the complex, changing world they will inherit in the future.

CHAPTER 9

Walking Alongside the Learner Through a Teacher-Designed Curriculum

A Study of "Change" in Yvonne's Prekindergarten Classroom

This chapter depicts a teacher-designed study that flows from the teacher's observations and responsiveness to the interests of the class. It shares the work of Yvonne Smith, a pre-K teacher at Central Park East 1 Elementary School, a public elementary school in East Harlem, New York City. Video images of Yvonne's classroom can be found at highqualityearlylearning.org/pre-k-videos/.

ORGANIZING THE CLASSROOM FOR ACTIVE LEARNING

Yvonne's classroom is organized into activity centers that feature areas for dramatic play, blocks, library, math, science, drawing and writing, painting, art and construction, sand and water play, playdough/clay, cooking, sewing, and a pet guinea pig.

Yvonne stresses the importance of this organization for supporting children's active learning, collaboration, and agency:

> The classroom is organized and set up so that the children can be as independent as possible. There are spaces for them to work in pairs, small groups, and a whole group. And the shelves and everything are labeled so that the children can get what they need and also clean up on their own.

Daily Choice Time Fuels Curriculum

A daily schedule frames the work and serves as a predictable guide for the children. Central to the schedule is choice time, to which an hour is dedicated each day. Based on understandings that choice motivates learning

(Brophy, 2013; Cordova & Lepper, 1996; Stipek, 2002), Yvonne gives children the opportunity to choose where they go. She explains:

> From the first day of school we have [choice time]. We ask the children, "Where would you like to work?" . . . And that says to them that we, the adults in the classroom, feel that they are capable of choosing where and how they want to work. . . .
>
> [The children] are physically acting on materials. It's not, "I talk, you listen, you repeat back." But, "You are discovering, you are sharing with your peers," and the role of the teachers is to support them in doing that. My job . . . is to support them to ask questions they obviously have, questions they may have that they do not necessarily ask, but by their actions we can see them asking, and questions that I think are important for them to ask.

CONNECTING TO CHILDREN'S INTERESTS AND QUESTIONS

Curriculum in Yvonne's classroom is created by connecting to and building on children's understandings, interests, questions, and needs.

> When I look at good early childhood curriculum, I look at it and say, "How can I bring this in in a way that will cover the things that are appropriate for 3's, 4's, and 5's to know, but do it in a way that absolutely walks alongside where the children are?"

Yvonne begins this process of connecting to children's understandings, interests, questions, and needs in the fall with the theme of "change." She explains:

> If people ask me what are we studying, I always say "change" because the children are new to the school. . . . In the beginning of the year, we talk about the things that are the same and different, and so right from the beginning I am asking them to think about, to observe, and to notice. And there is something in that word "notice" that says to kids it is more than just "tell me what you see," but "tell me what you have thought about and what you are beginning to have questions about and think about." . . . And as I hear what they say and how they look at things, I am getting a sense of who they are as thinkers and learners.
>
> In the classroom there are lots of books and concrete materials that . . . we begin exploring. . . . We spend time in the park and in the yard around our school, and the kids observe what's happening, and they notice the seasonal changes. They have questions about how and why it happens . . . trying to figure out and build a context for what

> is happening to them now, what they've noticed has happened before, and what they know is going to happen in the future. And as I see how they do things and what questions come up for them, I get an idea about how to support them in learning more, answering the questions that they have, and also provisioning for the things that they need to know.

How the Study of Change Progressed

The study of change progressed as the weeks went by and the leaves changed colors and fell from the trees. The class went apple picking and noted yet another change—from seed to apple. Later, a pumpkin was brought into the classroom. After carving it into a jack-o-lantern, the children observed what happened to it as time went by. They noticed how it began to shrivel, how liquid began forming in it, how mold grew, and how what the children called "caterpillars" (actually, flies) began to live inside.

Figure 9.1. Pumpkin Photo

They learned vocabulary words such as "decay" and "decomposition." They made hypotheses about what was causing these changes, realized there was a cycle of change happening within, and had discussions about whether they should throw the rotting pumpkin away. One child suggested that they put it out in the school's garden. The class agreed, and they took it there, checking on it regularly as it continued to decay. Through this investigation, they learned about another cycle of change—that the pumpkin would eventually merge with the soil and feed it. Through the experience, the class collectively constructed an understanding of composting.

Meanwhile, an uncut pumpkin remained at the nature center in the classroom. In class meetings, the children reflected on why that pumpkin stayed intact and did not rot. Those conversations, continuing over the winter, eventually brought the class to another study of what can be done to keep bodies healthy. "That's why these things stay here," explained Yvonne. "It's not a one-shot deal and then we're done with it. It's 'Let's leave it and see what questions arise and what we'll come back here to notice.'"

TEACHING TO SUPPORT HOW CHILDREN LEARN

Despite changes in standards and curricula over the years, Yvonne believes that the ways in which children learn remain constant.

> There is a lot of talk about curriculum and where it comes from. Right now, it is the Common Core (Common Core State Standards, 2015). But while curriculums come and go, your basic three-, four-, and five-year-old hasn't changed that much. The world has changed and the world that they live in has changed, and what they come knowing and having experienced has changed. But how they go about figuring things out and asking questions really hasn't changed. It is important for me to remember that and to hold on to that because children still need to have the materials, the time, and the support in making discoveries on their own and sharing those discoveries with others. We need to truly walk alongside them and support them in this.

To help children "figure things out" and "make discoveries on their own," Yvonne uses a range of strategies. These include the following: encouraging problem solving, inviting children to take notice of what is around them, querying children about how they arrive at what they know, and infusing skills into hands-on experiences.

Questioning to Encourage Children to Solve Problems

Questions play a big role in Yvonne's teaching. Her purpose is to nurture critical thinking and problem solving. She explains:

> In the block area, if someone's building keeps falling down, I'll say something like, "I notice that you're trying to get these blocks to

stand up. How else might you put them together so that they might stand up?" My question to them indicates that there are other ways of doing things. But I am not telling them what those other ways are. I'm expecting *them* to figure it out.

Inviting Children to Notice

Another way in which Yvonne supports learning is by inviting children to observe and notice. She asks:

> What do you notice when the red happens to mix with yellow or the blue happens to mix with the red? [I ask this] so that they see that things are going to happen when paints come together and to see if they can figure out what it is. It may seem obvious to an adult that if you mix red and yellow you'll get orange, but if you are 3 or 4, that's a huge discovery. And [my goal is] that they can name it and . . . be able to make that same thing happen and have some control over it, and draw some conclusions about their actions with these materials.

The purpose, as Yvonne explains, is to emphasize that taking a close look is valuable work:

> It's amazing to me that [when] you tell kids to sit and take a close look at something . . . how carefully they look, how seriously they take the work of seeing what is there. Someone once said that "I never really understood a thing until I took the time to describe and notice it." I think the children are finding out that it takes coming back to things again and again, that this takes time, and that it is valuable work . . . to notice and look at similarities and differences and to be able to say what they are . . .

Reflecting on How You Know What You Know

Yvonne also helps children build knowledge by encouraging them to think about how they know what they know. This strategy aims to develop children's metacognition. She explains how this works:

> One of the things we do is talk about what day it is . . . "How do you know it is Monday? Or Tuesday?" In the beginning of the year some of the children would say, "My mommy told me." This showed that they know there are adults who can give them the information they need. But after a while I tell them that's not good enough. I ask, "How else do YOU know what day it is?" This makes them have to think

> about other ways of knowing. And some kids will say, "We are having art today" or "Today is all-school sing" or "It's boys' chorus day" or "Peggy the Storyteller is coming." . . . Then someone will notice that there is a pattern that repeats. And at that point . . . they are figuring out that there is a repetition and a routine in what our schedule is over the course of the day and the week.

Teaching Skills in the Context of Experiences

In the context of engaging experiences like the ones described above, Yvonne builds academic skills and knowledge (Snow, Burns, & Griffin, 1998; Zigler, Singer, & Bishop-Josef, 2004). She explains:

> [Learning to read and write is] embedded in and will come out of the things we do. . . . It comes from children's natural curiosity and their need to know. [For example], as children are documenting the things they are studying—the nests or the guinea pigs who live in our room—we [the adults] are assisting them to write what they see.

Figure 9.2 Guinea Pig Observation

BUILDING COMMUNITY IN THE CLASSROOM

Yvonne's support for children's skill development, critical thinking, and problem solving is used not only for academics. It is used to address disciplinary issues as well. She explains:

> Kids come to school to read, write, and do math. But they also come to school to interact with others in a group—to build a community. There is an African saying that you can't have two coins in a pocket without having some noise. So, there is always going to be some conflict and noise. The question is, what do you do about it? When buildings are falling in the block area, you look at it as a problem to be solved. When two children both want the same red truck . . . that is the same kind of problem to be solved. It is part of the learning that must happen. And just as I will say how else might you get this building to stand up . . . it's how else can we figure out how each of you can use this red truck without someone feeling that it's not fair? I want the children to talk about it and solve it. . . . My job is to make sure that there is fairness and that each one has a chance.
>
> There are times when things come up over and over again—it may be that someone has hit someone or someone refuses to clean up—and then we need to have a meeting and we need to talk about this because it isn't being resolved and we have to resolve it. The children learn that you have to talk to that person first and that you need to listen to him. I walk them through it. It is not enough for the child to say "I'm sorry" and then walk off because that "I'm sorry" doesn't mean anything. They learn that they are expected to address the issue of what they did and whether or not they are going to continue doing it.
>
> This time of the year—those things that have come up [at the beginning of the school year] are no longer coming up because the children are learning that this process [of problem solving] not only keeps those who are bringing the issues safe, it also keeps the others safe. And we talk about that: When you come to school do you want people to do things to you that you don't like? How are we going to keep each other safe and make this a place where we all want to be? We do this constantly in September and October so that [by November or December] . . . we have a process. It is wonderful to hear the kids talking with each other and walking themselves through and only coming to the adults when they have a problem.

A SCHOOL CONTEXT AND PROCESS TO SUPPORT LEARNING

The school where Yvonne teaches, from its inception, has been a community committed to a shared vision of learning. It is a context that has nurtured her growth and enabled her to find and sustain joy in her work. The joy comes not only from *what* is done, but also from *how* it is done. Yvonne's process of "walking alongside each learner"—helping children to ask and answer questions, to collaborate, to persevere, and to recognize their strengths—is powerful. It is about supporting children through a journey that focuses on each individual's process of becoming a learner. Yvonne explains the impact on her graduates:

> Children often tell us, "The thing I like about being in this school, is that it always is about *my* work. My work may not be the best, but it is mine, and I can get there in my way, supported by the teachers." And when our kids go on to other schools, people often note that our kids are the ones who ask interesting questions, who stick to things and don't give up, who can work with others, who—most notably—seem to love learning. When you think about what is important, what more than *that* can you want?"

CHAPTER 10

Observing, Assessing, and Using Information to Inform Teaching and Support Learning

Being able to truly "see" students requires that teachers learn to look and listen carefully and nonjudgmentally in order to understand who students really are, what they think, and how they make decisions. As part of a pedagogy for empowerment, Paolo Freire (2005) talked about the importance of preparing teachers for "reading" a class of students "as if it were a text to be decoded [and] comprehended" (p. 49), especially when teachers come from economic and cultural backgrounds substantially different from those of their students:

> Just as in order to read texts we need such auxiliary tools as dictionaries or encyclopedias, the reading of classes as texts also requires tools that can be easily used. It is necessary, for example, to observe well, to compare well, to infer well, to imagine well, to free one's sensibilities well, and to believe in others without believing too much what one may think about others. One must exercise one's ability to observe by recording what is observed. But recording should not be limited to the dutiful description of what takes place from one's own perspective. It also implies taking the risk of making critical and evaluative observations without giving such observations airs of certainty. All such material should be in constant analysis by the teacher who produces it, as well as by his or her students. (Freire, 2005, p. 49)

The effective teacher creates opportunities for learners to explore, question, hypothesize, and argue about ideas with others in contexts of active experiences. To do this well, teachers need to pay careful attention to the information contained within learners' responses, questions, conjectures, and comments. This information can then be used to guide instruction and to ask more questions and make suggestions until new levels of complexity

---

This chapter is adapted from a chapter in *The Heart of the Matter: Using Standards and Assessments to Learn*, by Beverly Falk (Heinemann Press, 2000). Used by permission.

have been mastered and others begin to take shape. Such a teacher assists, provokes, encourages, and provides the safety needed for the risk-taking of genuine learning to occur.

To effectively support children's learning in this way, teachers need to be constantly inquiring—through a wide range of lenses and perspectives—about what children know, how they know it, and what their strengths and vulnerabilities are. This approach to learning about learners' needs is best informed by multiple forms of direct evidence of learning that are collected in a variety of meaningful, real-life contexts over an extended period of time in the classroom (Darling-Hammond, Ancess, & Falk, 1995).

Information from such classroom-based assessments can reveal a wide range of information about children and their progress. In addition to showcasing children's accomplishments, these assessments can tap into complexities of learning that conventional testing methods are not able to show, and they can explore complexities of thinking that go beyond simply getting the "right answer" to, instead, revealing children's strategies and approaches to learning as well as the strengths on which they rely (Falk, 2000; Kamii, 1985; National Association for the Education of Young Children, 1987; National Association of School Psychologists, 2005; National Council of Teachers of Mathematics, 2013).

Through such formats as teacher-kept observations, student-kept records, actual samples of children's work, and input from children and their families, teachers can develop a unique portrait of each child as a learner. This accumulated information can help to plan appropriate learning experiences and curricula that are responsive to the needs of individuals as well as groups of children.

Classroom-based assessments such as these can be used to collect evidence of children's work in various disciplines at regular intervals over the course of the school year. This kind of information documents the growth and development of each child over time. It is useful information to inform teaching, to share with children and their families, and to pass on to successive teachers about what children have learned, what they can do, and what the particular strategies, strengths, styles, and interests are that children bring to their learning experiences.

Following is a brief description of the different formats that can be used to document children's progress. These provide teachers with occasions for reflection, learning, and communication that can influence their curriculum, instruction, and professional growth.

TEACHER-KEPT RECORDS

Teacher-kept records can include documented observations of children, inventories or checklists of their skill development, or notes from teacher–student conferences. Dated and entered into a child's records, they can be used to track children's developing understandings and skills and to inform teachers' summary judgements for end-of-year or semester reports.

Just as children learn in different ways, teachers also observe and record children's progress in a multitude of ways. The following are some different methods: jotting down observations on note cards or in an electronic format, using "stickies" that get pasted into a notebook at the end of the day, or carrying a notebook that has sections demarcated for each child in which quick notes can be entered during the course of the day and longer reflections noted during preparation periods, lunch, or after-school hours.

Some teachers keep their records by regularly jotting down general comments about children's ideas and approaches to learning. Some teachers focus on recording children's progress in relation to specific skills, content, or standards. Whatever the focus, when this is done regularly over time, information is compiled that, by the end of the school year, provides a substantial record of each child's growth.

Descriptive rather than evaluative language is an important feature of this kind of assessment. In contrast to evaluative language, which frequently focuses on the end product of learning and heavily bears the judgment of the observer, descriptive language focuses on *how* something happens, noting the process as well as the product. Descriptive language holds the judgement of the observer in abeyance, focusing instead on unpacking the details of *why* one might be led to make a particular evaluation of a particular student in a particular context at a particular time. The descriptions below illustrate the difference. Compare these statements about Stephen's progress found in this report card:

1. Stephen has an excellent vocabulary.
2. Stephen does outstanding work.
3. Stephen has excellent math skills.

with this version that was completed by his teacher after practicing her observation and documentation skills:

1. Stephen uses a rich variety of descriptive words in his writing.
2. Stephen works independently and intensely. He thinks critically, takes risks in putting forward new ideas, and is thorough in attention to details of presentation.
3. Stephen is fluid in his thinking about number concepts. He can generally find several solutions to a problem and is able to explain them to others in a clear way. (Falk, 2000)

This kind of feedback explains what makes Stephen's vocabulary and math skills "excellent" and what about his work warrants the characterization of "outstanding." It provides Stephen's teachers, as well as his family and himself, with a better understanding of *how* he does what he does.

When descriptions in this vein accumulate, they paint a picture of each child as a learner. This picture helps children, their families, and other teachers to recognize children's strengths so that they can build on them further and so that they can identify areas in need of support and make plans for how to address them.

Here are some guidelines for how to create descriptive, documented observations of learners that will inform and support teaching:

- Portray the actions and behaviors
- Leave out judgment
- Document only what you see; don't make assumptions about what you see
- Date everything
- Provide a context for the observation
- Document a full segment from beginning to end
- Look for what students *can* do, not just for what they can't do

In addition to helping us think about learners' progress systematically, documented observations also help to broaden our overall conceptions of what constitutes learners' different kinds of strengths. The more we observe, the more sensitized we become to the diversity of talents and abilities in the learners we serve. This enables us to recognize children's abilities that formerly may not have been apparent. We are helped to recognize and appreciate what Howard Gardner refers to as "multiple intelligences"—linguistic, musical, bodily, spatial, and social strengths in addition to the logical and numerical ones emphasized most often in schools (Gardner, 1983).

Noting and appreciating such differences leads us to think about curriculum and teaching in a different way too. We move away from standardized approaches to teaching, which require everyone to do the same thing in the same way, toward a differentiated instruction—one that provides different kinds of learners with different pathways to achieve mastery of important common concepts and skills.

In early childhood, anecdotal notes and checklists are a key form of assessment for children's learning. Some schools/centers/districts have designed their own formats that guide teachers about what to look for. Others use commercially available materials such as *Teaching Strategies Gold, Work Sampling System, or HighScope's COR Advantage*. The challenge of using materials of this sort is to do more than just check off listed grade-level qualities and behaviors and, instead, to actually *use* the assessment information gathered to reflect on the strengths and needs of each child and use this information to guide future teaching. When strategies are worked out for how to do this, many teachers report that they begin to see things they had not noticed before. They realize that as they collect evidence about their learners over time, they achieve a perspective of each child's unique growth and development that can inform instructional decisions for individuals as well the class as a whole.

STUDENT WORK SAMPLES

Work samples are another source of information that can provide important insights about children and their learning. Teachers can collect these for a variety of purposes—to chronicle the growth and development of each child in order to learn about the nature of the child as a learner, to demonstrate each child's "best work," or to document how children fulfill standards that are required by the school or district.

The purpose of collecting samples of what students do in a range of media from all discipline areas is much the same as the purpose that drives the process of teacher records such as anecdotal notes and checklists—to gather evidence that chronicles progress, uncovers the nuances of how children approach learning, and reveals children's strengths and recurring interests. For example, writing samples reveal much about where children are on the continuum of literacy development, while math journals demonstrate—through algorithms as well as narratives—how children's mathematical thinking is progressing. Drawings, paintings, or (as children get older) documentation of projects, research reports, and science experiments provide evidence of how children solve problems that cut across disciplines.

Figure 10.1. Child's Drawing of a Submarine

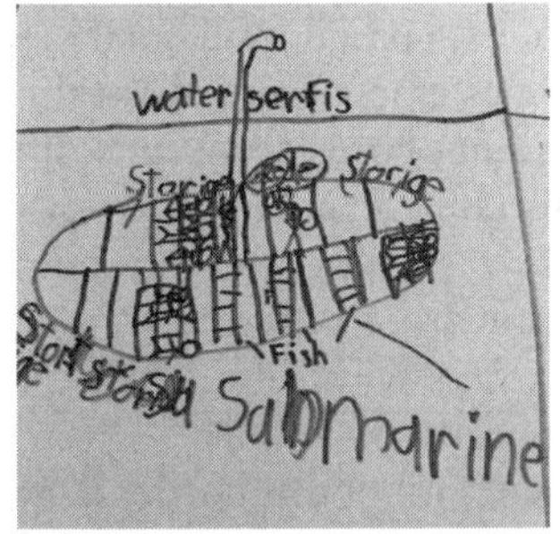

Photos of three-dimensional work (block buildings, woodworking, experiments, cooking, constructions) and of children engaged in activities with others (reading, tending to animals, sports, music, or dramatic play) give a sense of individuals' interests and learning styles. Dating these items as they are archived offers a view of children's progress over time. Combined with documented observations and checklists, these data help teachers note what children can do, what they understand, what their interests are, and what skills and understandings they need to work on to move forward with their learning.

STUDENT-KEPT RECORDS

Student-kept records are another helpful way to keep track of children's learning. Even children of the youngest ages can keep records of their reading and writing, their projects, and their reflections on their work. These ongoing records can serve as an organizer for the activities of the classroom, making it possible for teachers to move away from whole-group instruction as the only way of knowing what everybody is doing and enabling them, instead, to offer opportunities for independent and group work. When teachers ask children to articulate and keep track of what they have done and what they think, children develop a sense of responsibility, control, and ownership of their work and become more aware of their learning.

Many classrooms have children keep logs of their reading. Ranging in format from lists kept in notebooks, on oak tag bookmarks, or on teacher-designed forms, reading logs provide a way for children to keep track of what they have read, when they read it, and what they thought about what they read. This information provides the teacher with a sense of the range of genres and difficulty level of texts that the children are able to read.

Figure 10.2. Reading Record

_______________ 's Reading Record

Fall/Spring

Title: ____

Author: ____

Type of text: __fiction __nonfiction __poetry

I read this book:	Reading this book was:	My Opinion:
__ alone	__ easy	__ I didn't like it
__ with an adult	__ just right	__ It was okay
__ with a partner or group	__ hard	__ I liked it
		__ I loved it

Comments:

____

____

____

Student-kept records can be used for other subjects as well. Math journals or notebooks, for example, can be used to document what children can do and what they understand about important concepts and skills. Choice-time journals, in which children record what they worked on in centers during choice time, give them an opportunity to reflect on what they worked on, with whom, and what they learned or discovered.

In a similar way, project folders can be used to chronicle children's understandings in a variety of disciplines. Because projects offer the opportunity for learners to apply valued knowledge and skills, project work that is done in the course of classroom life can be a valuable learning experience in addition to being a demonstration of that learning. Teachers can use project folders to keep track of what children do during classroom time allocated for project work—the questions that arose, how they proceeded to answer those questions, and what they learned as a result. Examining project folders that are used in this way should provide understandings about what children know and what they can do that are useful in planning next steps for learning in a manner that is responsive to understandings and needs.

All of these student-kept records offer a means for children to work independently and to keep track of their learning so that they and their teachers get a sense of the continuity of their progress. Sharing these records during class time can also be valuable. When children show one another their work and discuss it, they not only build a sense of a learning community, they also clarify their thinking and stimulate new directions that can deepen and extend individual and group work.

DOCUMENTING THE LEARNING OF THE GROUP

Group learning can be further enhanced by recording on chart paper what took place in class discussions. These charts can be displayed sequentially on classroom walls, chronicling the learning of the class so that they can be used as a reference and reminder over time. The Reggio Emilia schools in northern Italy have publicized this way of documenting the learning journey of a whole class. Recording class learning in this way supports literacy by turning ideas into the symbols of writing. It also nurtures discussion, allows for the revisiting of powerful ideas, and serves as the basis for new ideas, projects, and partnerships (Edwards, Gandini, & Forman, 1998).

Figure 10.3. Classroom Chart

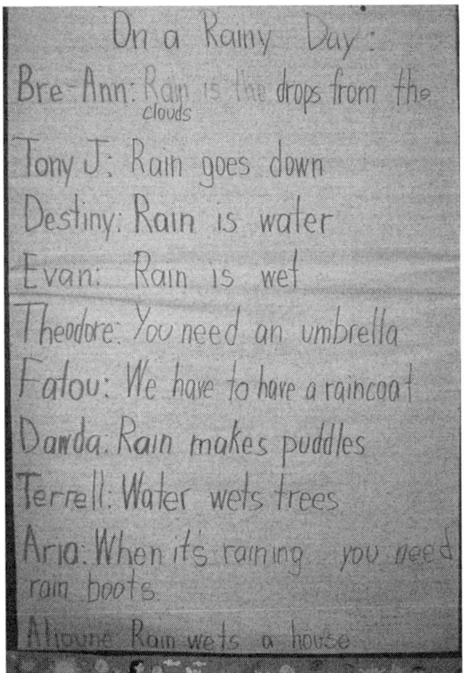

WEAVING ASSESSMENT INTO THE CURRICULUM: AN ITERATIVE CYCLE

When this combined information—teacher records, children's work samples, students' own records, and documentation of group discussions—is used in combination, it provides a fulsome picture of individuals' growth. Together this evidence can be used to inform and support teaching and learning.

The process of systematically gathering evidence, reflecting on its meaning, and using it to shape our teaching strategies offers us understandings of our students that can be used to make instructional decisions responsive to the unique needs, interests, and understandings of each learner. An evidence-based approach to teaching helps us make teaching a more professional act. It moves us away from personal feelings or intuition as a guide to our actions and toward a systematic process of using known facts to inform and support our instruction.

Figure 10.4. An Inquiry Cycle for Teaching

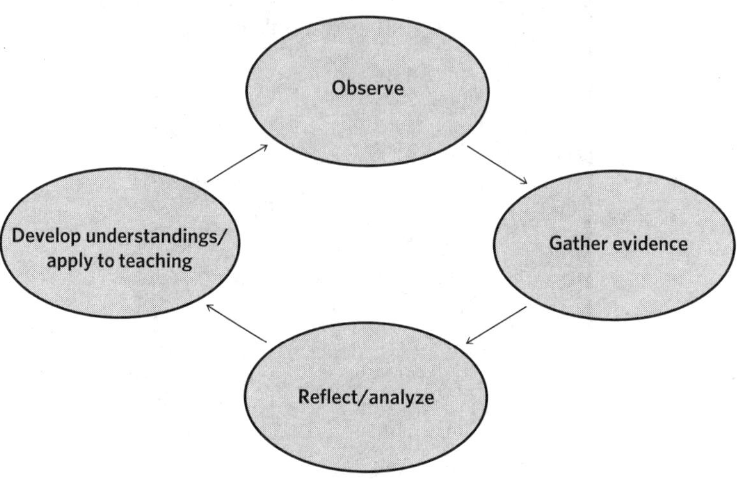

Working with Standards

Before discussing how to use evidence about children's learning to inform teaching, some discussion of standards and their use in early childhood is needed. In the last several decades, standards for what learners are expected to learn—at different ages and grades—have been articulated and adopted by states, districts, and professional associations. These are now used to guide curriculum throughout most pre-K–12 learning contexts. As discussed in an earlier chapter of this book, some of these standards are more appropriate for their targeted age groups than others. Those articulated for early childhood are considered by many to be problematic. Because early childhood is a period in which developmental variation is the norm, some argue that there should be no standards for young children at all—that young children should be allowed to grow at their own pace and in their own way. Others take a different stance: standards for the early years can be a helpful guide to teaching and learning *if* the variations that are characteristic of early childhood are acknowledged by articulating the standards for developmental stages rather than for grades and ages. This view is based on the widely acknowledged understanding that all children do not master the same skills and understandings at the exact same time but, rather, will typically master certain skills and understandings within a set period of development. For example, children generally move from being emergent to beginning readers or develop representational art between the ages of three and seven. So to require all children to be beginning readers by the end of kindergarten is not respectful of this developmental variation. As a result, the early childhood field has pushed back at efforts to narrowly define standards by age and grade and, instead, to guide teaching with a set of articulated expectations that children should be able to meet at different points on the developmental continuum. To date, this idea has not sufficiently made its way into assessment policy. There still is much advocacy work to be done.

So as we continually advocate for early childhood standards to stay true to what we know about how children learn, an important idea to keep in mind when working with standards is that there are certain things that children can and need to be expected to learn and to do. However, in order to support them in their learning, we must consider each child's needs, adjust to their understandings, and adapt to their questions, interests, and needs. Curriculum and instructional plans are thus more effective as maps of important sites on a journey than as itineraries that schedule places and activities for each hour of each day. While it can be helpful to have curriculum that serves as a conceptual guide to important knowledge and skills, there is no guide, plan, or syllabus that can effectively script how and at what pace each learner will learn. No guide can anticipate the surprises, the difficulties, the questions, or the misunderstandings that will arise. Neither can it predict in advance the fullness of the learning that will take place. And, certainly, no guide can guarantee that material will be learned just because it has been presented.

In other words, learning does not occur by simply mapping standards to curriculum and then performing specified teaching activities. Our teaching task is not about "covering" the standards but about ensuring that children understand and make sense of the ideas and skills represented by the standards. We need to "join with the learner," an idea discussed in earlier chapters of this book, to craft meaningful and purposeful curriculum that builds on children's prior understandings and skills.

Using Evidence to Guide Teaching

Throughout the course of our teaching we thus have to consider not only our curriculum and lesson plans but also their impact on our students. Only when we build into our plans a way to take into account what is happening with our students—through a continual gathering of evidence of what they understand and how they can actually apply their understandings—will we have a way to assess the effectiveness of our plans, to make adjustments to our teaching, and to heighten the likelihood that learning will occur.

This is why authentic assessments of children's learning are so helpful and central to effective teaching. The knowledge we gain of what learners know from the evidence we collect with these assessments can be an invaluable guide to our instruction. It gives us clues to what we need to do to help children gain mastery of skills and to ensure that they understand important concepts. It offers us insights about each learner's unique way of processing information and of making sense of the world. And it prevents us, when students have difficulties with their learning, from attributing these difficulties to some flaw in their intellect or their character. Rather, it focuses us on *our* responsibility to try to understand our learners' thinking, their issues, and their problems, and to keep searching for the keys to their learning until we can find ways to help them succeed (Elbow & Belanoff, 1986).

Use Multiple Forms of Evidence to Gain Knowledge of Children's Growth

Documented observations, samples of children's work, and student-kept records are all helpful ways to gain information about children's learning that can be used to inform next steps for teaching—what is often referred to as "formative" assessment. Additionally, summative assessments that gather evidence at the conclusion of a study—in the form of an on-demand task or common work sample that all children in the class produce—can provide information about how children have met the overall goals of a study, curriculum, or unit. Taken together, these multiple forms of evidence can provide a rich picture of each child as a learner.

Figure 10.5. Multiple Forms of Evidence of Learning

Teacher records	Student work	On-demand tasks/ common work sample
Observations	Reading logs	Essays
Inventories	Collections of • Writings • Drawings • Photos • Videos	Exhibitions
Checklists	Self-evaluations	Experiments
Conference notes		Multi-step problems
Collected information about children's ways of learning; about family, culture, and language		Artistic performances
		Projects
		Reports

Performance Tasks and Rubrics Offer Guidance to Learning

Performance tasks provide opportunities to learn what children know and can do in relation to different aspects of a study or disciplinary learning. For children in the older years of the early childhood continuum—kindergarten and the primary grades—performance tasks can be created to embody standards of different disciplines. These tasks can offer a child-friendly way for children to demonstrate expected knowledge and skills.

A rubric for the task lists the important qualities of the standards that are embodied in the task, describing what the qualities of the standards look like at different stages of development. It can help teachers determine the degree to which children are learning the standards. It can also be helpful for children in the older years of the early childhood span to use themselves, offering them a guide to the elements of high-quality work.

Rubrics can be holistic or analytic. They can be used for general or task-specific purposes. Holistic rubrics give overall descriptions of work that translate into a single score. An example is a score of 1 to 10 for a paper, project, or task.

In contrast, analytic rubrics offer separate descriptions for the different criteria of a task. Each criterion is assessed, and then these scores get added up to produce one overall score that assesses the entire performance. Different criteria can sometimes be given more weight than others based on their importance. An example of this kind of scoring is a skating competition, which usually evaluates skaters by combining separate scores for technical and artistic merit. This way of assessing performance is useful in clarifying expectations for different aspects of a task or performance.

Rubrics can be used for different purposes. This too is reflected in their design. They can be developed either to assess a specific task or to assess many tasks that represent a skill or body of knowledge. A task-specific rubric or scoring guide is useful for assessing how a student has met the unique criteria that are specified for a particular task. In contrast, a general rubric describes criteria or qualities for a more generic activity, such as reading. Reading scales, such as those used by Fountas and Pinnell (2016) to denote different levels of readers, are an example of a generic scale and can be used to monitor general progress in reading over time, across several pieces of work, using multiple products and performances.

Ensuring Reliability and Validity

When developing tasks and rubrics it is important to take care that realistic expectations guide the work. In formulating these expectations, it is important to consider long-range goals as well as what is developmentally appropriate and feasible to attain. Otherwise, standards may be set in such a way that disproportionate numbers of children fail to meet them. This is part of the case being made in arguments against using standards with young children: that young children are not meeting standards because there is something unreasonable about what the children are being asked to do. Careful consideration must be paid to this issue when crafting any standards and standards-based assessments. How this issue is addressed affects how valid and reliable any standards and assessments will be.

A useful way to ensure that any standards-based study, project, or assessment task is valid and maintains an appropriate balance between standards and reasonable expectations is to develop the rubric by continually cross-referencing expectations with children's work (see Figure 10.6). We also should bear in mind what we know about child development and what it tells us about what children can and should be able to do. The rubric should thus be designed as a continuum of learning from beginning to advanced, rather than as a set of arbitrary expectations. After the goals and expectations are set, it is important to consider children's work and review it for how it meets initial expectations. This evidence can then be used to help determine how reasonable the initial expectations are. Teachers need to ask questions such as, What expectations in the work do children seem unable to do? Are they unable to do it because we haven't taught it to them, we haven't taught it to them properly, or it is an inappropriate expectation at this point in their development?

These questions are important to consider when formulating expectations as well as when creating work plans and assessments. We need to work back and forth between standards, criteria, descriptions of performance, and student work.

Working in this way will help to ensure that our expectations, as expressed in our standards, our curriculum, and our assessment, are authentic and valid reflections of what students actually can do.

Reliability is also an important issue to address when developing standards-based assessments. A reliable assessment will provide a consistent view of student work. That means that if different people look at the work, they will evaluate it in a similar way. It also means that work completed by the same person at different times will be evaluated similarly by the assessment.

Figure 10.6. Process for Developing a Rubric

Articulate the standards that the task is assessing

↓

Spell out criteria for the task

↓

Describe performance for each criterion at different levels of performance

↓

EVALUATE AND SCORE STUDENT WORK

↑

Describe how student work meets task criteria

↑

Examine student work

↑

Gather student work

Assessment reliability and validity are particularly challenging to achieve with performance tasks that are to be used to influence decisions that involve high stakes such as grade retention or promotion. However, when developing assessments that are going to be used in the classroom primarily for instructional purposes, reasonable reliability can be reached by making sure that the assessment provides the following:

Criteria That Are Clear, Do Not Overlap, and Are Specifically Linked to Standards. Make sure not to confuse *standards-based criteria* with *technical requirements* for how products and performances are to be produced. Examples of criteria that relate to standards are "uses details to support ideas" or "makes connections." Examples of technical requirements that should be avoided in a rubric are "gives one detail from the story" or "uses 3 conventionally spelled words."

Scales That Make Clear Distinctions Between Levels. Each level of the rubric should be descriptive of work as it develops from the earliest to the most advanced stage.

Performance Descriptions That Are Specific, Observable, and Can Be Documented. Make sure that what is described in the rubric can actually be seen in the work (Harris & Carr, 1996).

Figure 10.7. Rubric Example

Task: Ask each child to sort the nature objects (pinecones, acorns, chestnuts, leaves, twigs) into groups. (The groups can be based on size [big/medium/small], color [light/dark], shape [round/straight/pointy], or some other category [like smooth/rough]). Ask each child to explain the sorting criteria.

Goals/Objectives	Meets the challenge	In process or developing	Not yet or beginning
Completes the task—is able to sort the objects into distinct categories	The categories are clear and all/most objects fit in them correctly	The categories are made but some objects do not match the categories	Little or no understanding of different categories and little to no matching of objects to them
Explains the categories	Is able to clearly define the categories and clearly explain why and how different objects fit	Is able to state the categories but explanation of how and why objects fit in is not clear or full	Is not able to explain the categories or how and why objects fit in

Working with standards-based assessments over time can stimulate development among teachers and learners about common understandings and expectations about how children develop along a continuum of progress as well as about what constitutes quality work. Teachers start to acquire shared meanings and a common language that provides consistency and coherence across the school. Learners get clearer images of expectations and become more adept at monitoring their own learning. The clearer the standards, the better guided young learners are to reach them, and the higher the quality of work that is ultimately produced.

COMMUNICATING ABOUT CHILDREN'S LEARNING WITH FAMILIES AND COMMUNITIES

How children are progressing in their learning, as demonstrated by all of the different ways of collecting evidence of their learning discussed here, can be shared through a variety of formats.

Narrative Reports

A narrative report, written about a learner by the teacher(s), is a teacher's synthesis of a child's progress based on evidence collected throughout the school year. Narrative reports take care to be descriptive and stay away from judgments and evaluator language. They are based on teachers' analysis of anecdotal notes and children's work. Some schools send narrative reports home to families and then use these as the basis for discussion at parent/family conferences.

Report Cards

Report cards have traditionally been used to inform families and schools systems about children's learning. Moving away from letter grades or evaluations such as "excellent, good, fair, or poor," many school communities have, instead, created report cards that describe learners' progress in relation to the standards of their districts or states. Other schools and districts have transformed their reporting systems to reflect learners' progress along a continuum of development, such as those articulated for literacy by Fountas and Pinnell (2016) or by the *New York State Early Literacy Profile* (New York State Education Department, 1999; see www.p12.nysed.gov/ciai/ela/pub/elp1.pdf). Evaluations of individual learners are made by considering where children are on the developmental continuum, how much progress they have made in relation to where they were at the time of the last assessment, and what is a reasonable expectation for them, taking into consideration their age and grade. A complex set of factors—child development understandings and pedagogical content knowledge in the disciplines—lead to the formulation of *reasonable expectations* for where students should be by what grade.

Conferences, Exhibitions, Museums

No written word can ever fully capture the power of a lived experience. Some ways to share the richness of children's learning beyond what written reports or grades can do are home–school conferences, student exhibitions, and "museum" presentations of student work.

Home-School Conferences. Home–school conferences can be an avenue for teachers to learn about families and for families to learn about their children's learning at school. A home–school conference is a meeting between the teacher and the significant people in the child's life (the child can also be included). It is a scheduled event to discuss the progress of the child as well as any questions and concerns family members may have. The child's work is on hand so that families have firsthand contact with the concrete evidence of the child's learning. In the process of examining this work together, teachers, the children, and their families can see and discuss how the child is progressing.

Home–school conferences can strengthen trust between home and school. They demonstrate to the learner that there are no behind-the-scenes secrets—that nothing will be done "to" her or him without frank, collaborative discussions concluding in mutual consent. They also help families understand the school's goals, purposes, and expectations while providing opportunities for families to share their perspectives, expectations, and dreams for their child's learning as well as their understandings of who their child is. This mutual sharing increases the trust needed for a sense of community to flourish in a school.

Exhibitions/Museums. Another way to communicate about what is involved in children's learning is through creating exhibitions or "museums" designed for children to display and explain their work. In a "museum," a classroom is temporarily transformed into exhibits that incorporate the learning from a completed study—children-made books, experiments, artwork, constructions, puppet shows, videos, or musical performances. Children share what they have learned as they display and explain their work to classmates, schoolmates, family members, and school faculty (Falk, 2008).

Figure 10.8. Museum

These ways of sharing about learners' progress, carried out in many schools that serve children and families from different backgrounds, strengthen the capacities of the entire community to engage in and support powerful learning. The next chapter offers an image of how this can be done and how children's learning is shared through an all-school museum.

Using Assessment to Inform Teaching and Support Learning

The Bronx River Study in Jessica and Andrene's 1st-Grade Classroom

This chapter showcases how teachers use assessment practices to learn about their students, support their learning, and share what they know and can do. It describes the work of Andrene Robinson and Jessica Lawrence, 1st-grade coteachers in an ICT classroom (mixed general and special education) at the Bronx Community Charter School, a public K–8 charter school in the Norwood section of the Bronx, New York City. Video images of Jessica's and Andrene's classroom can be found at highqualityearlylearning.org/first-grade-videos/.

CONTEXT/BACKGROUND

At the Bronx Community Charter School, active learning through projects and other hands-on experiences extends throughout the grades. To create a sense of community throughout the school, the school year begins with a 6-to-8-week all-school study. Each grade studies a different aspect of the same topic, engaging in projects that are showcased at an "All-School Museum" at the study's conclusion. When the school first moved into its current building, the beginning-of-the-school-year-study was about the new building. Each grade studied a different aspect of the building—one grade studied the lunchroom, another the lighting system, another the elevator, and so on. The following year, the school decided to explore what was directly behind their building—the Bronx River and its surrounding forest. Every grade selected a part of the forest to study, with the 1st grade choosing to investigate the river and the animals that live in and around it.

INCORPORATING CHILDREN'S INTERESTS, QUESTIONS, AND UNDERSTANDINGS INTO CURRICULUM PLANNING

Before the school year began, the teachers spent time—first as a whole school, then as a grade, and finally as an individual class—crafting a plan about the big ideas and issues that would be involved in their study. As part of their planning, they consulted the skills and standards for their grade that were required by the state, making sure that they wove them into an overall plan.

The initial draft plan was based around guiding questions that touched on big ideas and incorporated key skills and standards. Guiding questions were developed weekly—one week the plan was to study the parts of the river, the next week the plan was to get into studying the animals that lived in and around the river, the following week was about exploring the different animals' habitats, and so on—with tentative dates set for where they might study certain things. But because the teachers believe that building on children's interests, questions, and understandings supports the children to be involved and engaged in their learning, the teachers stayed flexible and open and allowed the children to shape the study's twists and turns. For example, as the animal study began and the children read about different animals living in and near the river, the children got to choose what animals they wanted to study in depth. At a class meeting they constructed a chart of river animals and divided up into groups to study different ones.

Figure 11.1. Animal Chart

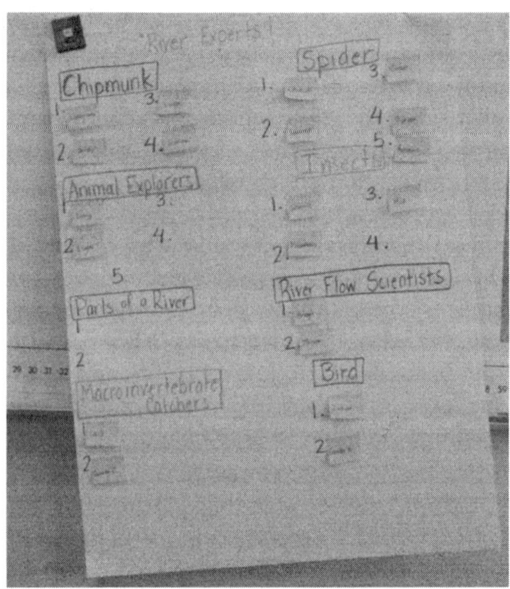

Some children chose birds, others chose spiders, still others chose worms. As Andrene explained:

> We wouldn't say, "Okay, we are going to study the fish, and the bird and the chipmunk and the squirrel . . ." We won't do that. We have to wait and see. We know we are going to study animals. We knew that learning about habitats is in the Common Core Standards. And that's great 'cause it gives us sort of an idea of where we are going to go, and as teachers we can plan in that way. We knew that animals and habitats were the big umbrellas, and then everything else was sort of, like, the kids are going to choose where we go with this.

Questions that arose in the course of the work led to investigations not originally predicted. For example, a question from a child about how fast the river flows led to an experiment at the river where the children counted how long it took for a leaf that they dropped off of a bridge to travel to a rock further downstream. As Jessica explained:

> Our trips to the river become the curriculum and you have to take it from there. It's almost like a river: It forms at the source and then it comes off into little tributaries and the kids are the tributaries.

INFUSING SKILLS AND CONTENT KNOWLEDGE INTO THE STUDY

The teachers in this 1st-grade classroom have clear understandings of the range of their students on the developmental continuum—in regard to their social/emotional capacities as well as their grasp of the skills and knowledge outlined in the standards for their grade. While these teachers keep developmental understandings primary, they use the standards as a guide for their instruction and intentionally infuse these into any study or project that they do. Andrene explains how skills and content knowledge of the standards are addressed in the Bronx River study:

> Any read-aloud that we would do would be focused around the river or around animals. If I was going to do a nonfiction lesson in literacy, I would try to pick not just any nonfiction book but something that is going to be about frogs or river animals or something that is going to connect to the study. Even the writing—we had a lot of time when they were writing about going to [the] river. That drove a lot of our writing time. The study is always looming around in everything that we do.

Jessica adds:

> For example, to help the children reinforce counting skills, in one of our trips to the river we did an experiment about river flow: Off of a bridge over the river, the kids threw a leaf and counted how long it took to be carried by the river's flow to a particular rock. I knew that it wasn't going to be a timed accuracy for the river flow, but I knew that the kids were going to get a lot out of it because they were going to get practice in counting. They got experience hearing the numbers, saying the numbers, going in order. And a lot of them need that help. Other kids know numbers up to 100; some kids don't. So just hearing kids say numbers in order is something they need to do every day.

The Bronx River study provided lots of opportunities for other content and skill work as well. For example, through their trips and readings the children gained science knowledge as they learned about the river's source, how the river flows, and the riverbank. As Andrene notes:

> When they go out there, they apply what they've learned in the classroom. They will realize that "this is the riverbank we're walking on," or "that's the riverbed we read about. . . ."

And through the hands-on experiences of building different animal habitats, such as a spiderweb, the children learned such concepts and vocabulary as "arachnids" and "macroinvertebrates."

Figure 11.2. Spiderweb

By examining spiders up close, they came to understand that the organisms they were studying had eight legs. By constructing different bird's nests, they came to understand how very small the house sparrow is. And they gained more math experience and understandings as they used rulers to measure an actual house sparrow egg.

Figure 11.3. Bird's Nests

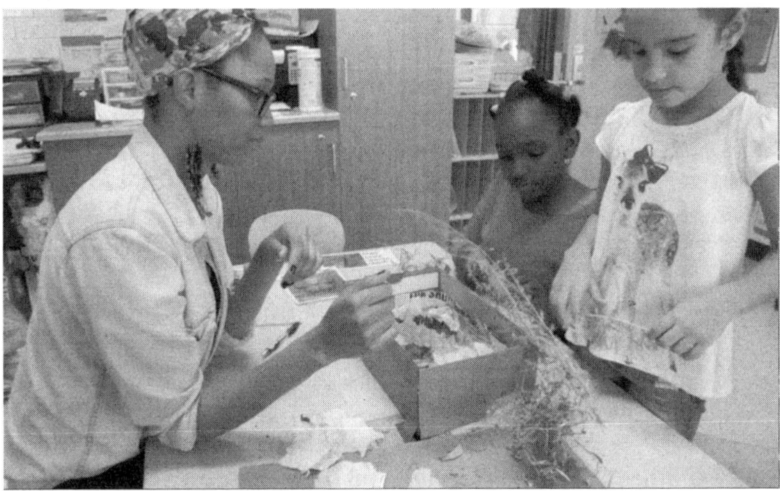

The Bronx River theme was seen in other areas of work as well. For instance, children made trees and bridges and rivers in their Lego and block building. Even the yoga done by the class during break times was influenced by the study when the children learned a river pose.

SHARING THE STUDY THROUGH AN ALL-SCHOOL MUSEUM

At the study's conclusion, the children created a "museum" to share their completed work with one another, with others in the school, and with their families. Since the Bronx River was the focus of study in all the grades of the school, each class presented and the entire community participated. The event was held at the river, where visitors could view and try out the different projects the children had made. Charts and murals inspired by the study were displayed while river-related songs, dances, and yoga poses were also presented.

Figure 11.4. Bronx River Museum

All the students wore name tags around their necks indicating that they were an "expert" on a particular issue related to their study. The tags for the 1st-graders displayed their names and a question about a particular river animal or animal fact. For example, one boy's tag said, "Ask me: What food do worms like to eat?" His answer was that "worms like bananas." Another child, a new immigrant and emergent bilingual (English language learner), had a name tag that showed he was a spider expert. Although communicating in English was still difficult for him, he had learned many technical terms related to spiderwebs as well as the names of the different parts of the spider like "abdomen" and "cephalothorax." When a crowd of 6th-grade students came to visit his exhibit and they asked him the question on his name tag, despite his shyness and nervousness about speaking in front of people, he was able to share with them everything he knew. The big kids were so impressed, they gave him high fives and were overheard saying, "Wow, he knows so much about spiders!"

In these ways, the Bronx River study provided an engaging way to support children's acquisition of academic skills and disciplinary content knowledge. And this learning did not end with this one study. It was revisited throughout the remainder of the school year. For example, the pollution of the water system in Flint, Michigan, which was in the news later that year, provided another opportunity for the class to continue their study of water and extend their knowledge. They went on to learn about the sources from which communities obtain the water they drink, how it is filtered, and other related information. So it wasn't just teaching one thing and then being done with it; rather, these concepts and skills were woven throughout the year.

CLASSROOM CENTERS AND MATERIALS

The way in which the classroom environment is set up is critical for facilitating the kind of work that takes place in the Bronx River study. Jessica and Andrene's 1st-grade classroom is organized into areas that each have a table and shelves stocked with materials. Additional tables are used as universal areas that can be interchangeably used for any activity. There is a meeting area with a smart board, a library, and areas for math/manipulatives, science, blocks, drawing/writing, construction, and other materials like Legos and puzzles.

Every day the classroom schedule includes several choice times. Some choice times are open-ended—for the children to choose the activities in which they want to be involved. Some choice times are assigned to a particular focus—a reading time, a math time, and so on. As the children engage with the available materials, they often work on skills and develop understandings related to the current theme of study. For example, in the block area they might re-create the bridge they saw on a trip to the river. Or, in the area where there is painting, drawing, writing, and paper construction, they draw birds and paint the trees they have seen in the forest surrounding the river. Jessica explained:

> We want the kids to see that learning is a hands-on experience. You have to engage with it. You have to be active in your learning. . . . If we are doing a story problem, use these cubes. . . . Put your hands on something. Re-create what you just heard. . . . [For example, the question,] "What is something we can build that we saw at the river today?" led to kids building the bridge, the trees, and a squirrel out of Legos.

MANAGING THE DISCIPLINE NEEDED FOR ACTIVE LEARNING

Running an effective active learning classroom requires cooperation and discipline from all members of the community. From the very first day of school, Andrene and Jessica start to develop a culture in the classroom to support this. The first several weeks of school are spent orienting the children to the classroom and routines. The teachers give the children a tour around the room, show them where the materials are, and discuss how to take care of the materials. They teach the children to use silent signals for such events as going to the bathroom and getting water. The focus is on how to be independent and to do things for themselves.

From the very beginning, the teachers try to establish an understanding with the children that the class is a community, a family; everyone needs to take care of each other. They ask children to think about how they would like someone to treat them. They do a lot of modeling to help the children develop a clear sense of what that looks like. They have the class make "promises" that are then written on a chart that hangs in the room. Signed by everyone in the class, this promise list is referenced constantly: "Are you taking care of your teaching? Are you taking care of your learning? Are you taking care of each other? What does that look like?"

Before sending the children off for project work, the teachers remind everyone: "If you are going to go and get scissors, you walk like this. If you need something from a friend, don't grab it from them. You have a voice. We want to hear your voice. You can raise your hand and you will be heard. We are going to have to help each other."

DIFFERENTIATING THE CURRICULUM FOR ALL STUDENTS

Jessica and Andrene's classroom is an Integrated Co-Teaching (ICT) classroom—a type of special education service in which one general education teacher and one special education teacher work together in the same classroom to support and teach children with and without identified disabilities together. Because of this setup, children in the class frequently do not do the same things. The established class culture is that people are different, they have different needs, and therefore they are often engaged in different things. The teachers regularly reinforce that understanding so the children know that "you may not have the same job as somebody else, but right now you're with this group and this is your job. You may have to wait, but you are going to get your turn to get help from a teacher." It takes a while to establish, but the children get better and better at this each week.

KEEPING TRACK OF CHILDREN'S LEARNING

To ensure that everyone is progressing in their work, especially in a classroom where children are at different levels of development—both socially/emotionally and skillwise—the teachers employ a range of strategies to keep track of the children's learning. One important source of information is observational notes. Although both teachers make a point of knowing all of their students, they each have a set of children that they take primary responsibility for assessing and for deciding on what their next instructional steps will be. Every week the teachers sit together to share their notes so that they get to know everyone well, and to reflect, schedule, and plan together. A system of clipboards for each child's progress in different discipline areas creates a comprehensive system of keeping track.

Figure 11.5. Keeping Track

For example, every time the children write a piece, they put the published work in their writing bins. The teachers review these to see what kinds of strategy groups they need to pull together and what additional skill work is still needed to be done. They do a lot of looking at the children's math work as well—to determine what the children understand, what they still need to work on, and what are the next steps for instruction. One of the teachers may pull a group out to work on a special skill or issue while the other teaches a lesson to the rest of the class.

Launching the school year with the Bronx River study helps to start this process of getting to know children well and creating a baseline of understanding about each child. It helps the teachers learn about the children's strengths, their needs, and their ways of working. As Jessica explains:

> The Bronx River study is the most amazing way to get to know kids as learners. I can see through this work what kids are going to be really benefiting from project work, what kids are going to be more independent in that area, what kids need more support there, what kids needs help with writing, what kids need help with reading skills or partnership work. I can see so many things this way. Through this study, we get to know who they are.

SHARING THE LEARNING WITH FAMILIES

Narrative reports are used to share information with the school and families about children's progress. Instead of report cards with letter grades like most of us were used to getting in school, Andrene and Jessica and the other educators at their school use observational notes and samples of children's work to fill out checklists that examine all the developmental areas—cognitive/academic (math, literacy, science, etc.) as well as social/emotional (work habits, what the child is like as a learner, and the child's strengths, interests, goals, and areas of struggle). As Jessica explains:

> It's sort of like writing a book about each one of your students. Although it is challenging and time-consuming, I think that it helps me really get to know them, too. As I sit there and reflect on moments that each child has had that have shown me what the child is like—for example, "wow—so and so was so caring when I saw her helping her friend"—I'll write that in the report and paint that picture for the parent.

The approximately two-page reports are completed three times per year—November, March, and June—for each child. They get sent home to families and are followed up by a family conference, where the children's areas of strength and those in need of more attention are discussed.

Every member of the family—it can be grandpa, grandma, brother, sister—who wants to attend the conference is invited. It usually starts off with a presentation by the child. The child gets to choose how to do it—whether to show their family members a strategy they're working on in reading and read them a book, or read them a published piece, or show them a math game, or share an observational drawing from the Bronx River study. Conference participants respond, and then the child leaves the tables and goes to work with Legos or other materials while the adult family members talk with the teacher.

The narrative reports for each child travel with them throughout their entire school career. They are sent to the teachers who will be working with the children in the next school year, which enables the teachers to really see what kind of student each child is. This process is an intimate way of communicating with families and other teachers about who that student is, offering authentic glimpses of each child as they work throughout the school day.

SCHOOLWIDE SUPPORTS

The kind of intentional and reflective teaching that has been described here in this close-up of Andrene's and Jessica's classroom is enabled by a supportive school environment, led by the school's codirectors, who are always giving feedback and who are constantly thinking of ways that the teachers can put their heads together to work as a team. Each classroom teaching team has a weekly meeting with one of the leaders to help them think about how they can strengthen their coteaching relationship, how they can make a plan for the week that can highlight differentiation, or how to support those children who are really struggling. The leaders also regularly check in with the teachers to make sure that they feel supported. As Jessica explains:

> [The school leaders] are not hovering over us and going, "make sure you are doing this, keep your pacing on point, you need to be here in math." They're not doing that because I think that they know that is not conducive to our teaching and not conducive to the kids' learning. They trust us a lot as teachers. They know that we need openness and the same flexibility we give our kids to get what they need.

The teachers also have the support of other school staff: literacy coaches, math coaches, and intervention teachers who will also come in and say, "What are you doing? How can I support you?" It can be about a specific study like the Bronx River study, about specific goals they have set for the students, or about ideas the teachers want to develop for the next content study. Jessica continues to explain:

> We meet once a month with a coach. It's a cycle. I had it today. I started a cycle today where I met with our literacy coach. She comes in once a month, but she's with me for three days. We have a really intense meeting about something that I'm wondering about in literacy and she'll have a big professional development with me on it for about two hours, and it's really intense and we'll practice some strategies and some skills with kids, and then she comes into the classroom with me the following day and she watches me do it, and she coaches me while I am doing the thing that we just practiced the previous day. The third day we are reflecting on it—we're thinking about where do we want to go next? Was this helpful? What still feels confusing? So, it guides you into the next step. It's not like "now we're going to learn something completely new." It's so funny, 'cause now as I am reflecting on it, our coaches do exactly with us what we do with the kids. So, I think us being able to have time to sit and reflect with the coaches, with the codirector, with each other, and then with the students, it's just a constant state of thinking about who you are as a learner, who you are as a teacher, and who we are as a community at this school.

Even more people are available to support the teachers if they feel a need for yet other eyes to look at their work. Teachers often touch base with their colleagues in the grades adjacent to theirs—for Andrene and Jessica in the 1st grade this means the kindergarten teachers and the 2nd-grade teachers—and sometimes they even consult with the teachers in the upper grades. To do this, the school frees them up from their classroom to walk around to the other classrooms so that they can look at how those classrooms are set up and what tools the teachers are working with. Keeping in touch with how the children move through the grades in these ways is important to ensure continuity for everyone's learning.

Additionally, there are staff meetings at the school that take place twice a week. On Mondays there is a meeting where the staff does a lot of thinking and reflecting about how things are going schoolwide: How is the lunchroom acting, how is recess going, is something else needed there? And then on Friday afternoons the children get dismissed at 2:00 P.M. and the whole staff has a 2-hour professional development experience. These sessions touch on many different issues. Sometimes it's academic based; sometimes it's more social based; sometimes the teachers get to use the time to plan or to work on their classroom environments. During the period of the Bronx River study, the school was doing a lot of identity work, thinking about gender, race, and things that are relevant and current in our society; how that relates to the students; and how it impacts teaching. Andrene sums up the impact of these supports:

> I think it helps us. We do reflect a lot here. We get a lot of time to reflect with each other, by ourselves, as a staff. I think it helps us to push the kids and ourselves forward. Because we share the same philosophy and the way we are with kids, it just makes for a really great environment. Our joint planning and reflecting really rub off on the kids and our energy because they see us as a team and they see us as a family together, and so it makes it a really good place to be and to learn because we are all happy to be here together.

Part III

STRATEGIES FOR SUPPORTING CHILDREN'S LEARNING

CHAPTER 12

Focusing on Literacy

Throughout all of the experiences of an active learning classroom, development of disciplinary content knowledge and skills are taking place. While this book is not intended to, nor is it able to, provide an in-depth guide to the pedagogical content knowledge of all of the disciplines, literacy development is addressed here because literacy learning takes place throughout all learning experiences. In addition, I demonstrate how literacy, and by example other disciplines—like mathematics, science, social studies, and the arts—can be infused into the everyday life of a classroom. Despite the differing pedagogical approaches that are unique to different content areas, all of the disciplines share a common foundational principle: that meaningful and purposeful contexts offer rich opportunities for young children to be exposed to, learn about, and have opportunities to practice important content knowledge and skills.

LITERACY DEVELOPMENT IS A CONTINUUM

While learning does not happen in strict hierarchical stages, we do know that there is a general pattern of stages or milestones that each child progresses through at his or her own speed in the journey to developing disciplinary content knowledge (Piaget, 1952, 1970; Piaget & Inhedler, 1969). To best support children as they proceed along the developmental continuum, educators need to offer plentiful opportunities—both formal and informal, direct and indirect—for children to have rich and active experiences at every stage of development.

READING DEVELOPMENT

Learning to read is a naturally occurring process that unfolds as children try to make sense of the print found everywhere in the world—from books read to them at home and school, to signs on the street, in stores, and so on. The key to strong literacy development is experiencing a rich language and literacy environment that connects to the learner and his or her real-life experiences (Dickinson & Tabors, 2001). The more that adults talk with children, read to children, sing with children, and engage them in interesting experiences, the more that sound, print, and vocabulary awareness will develop (National Research Council, 1998; Snow, 1983). In the following sections, the elements of learning to read are described in brief.

Sound Awareness

Awareness of different letter sounds (phonemic awareness) and recognition of different sound structures (phonological awareness) are developed through songs and rhythmic games (clapping games, name games). Ongoing experiences with rhymes and playing with words eventually help children learn that changing the letter or syllable will change what the word says. This, of course, is facilitated by intentional supports from teachers and other adults (Adams, Foorman, Lundberg, & Beeler, 1998).

Phonics and Print Awareness

Recognition that different sounds are connected to different letters is called *phonics awareness*. Recognition of familiar words is called *print awareness*. Children begin to recognize print on familiar food containers and classroom labels (especially their own name). Adults can help by pointing out the names of labels and words that are important and useful to children.

Vocabulary

Hearing and trying out a lot of new words is a big part of learning to read. The more children are read to and spoken with, and the more they read independently, the more their vocabulary develops. Studies have actually correlated vocabulary development with reading and overall school success (Snow, 1983; Weizman & Snow, 2001).

Reading Comprehension

Learning to read is not just about recognizing sounds, letters, and words. It, most importantly, is about understanding the meanings of the printed words. So it is critical for teachers and the adults in children's lives to discuss the texts they read to make sure that the children are understanding what is being read and that they develop models of how readers make meaning as they read. Interactive reading and storytelling, interspersed with questions and comments, can support comprehension. Also supportive are opportunities for children to retell stories using puppets, props, and skits, as well as to draw or write about what they have read. However, because comprehension has so much to do with background knowledge about the world, one of the key ingredients of strong comprehension is having exposure to rich experiences in the world (Willingham, 2017).

Strategies That Support Reading

Daily reading with children is one of the most important activities teachers and parents/caregivers can do to support literacy. There are many strategies in use during reading—not just phonetic (recognizing the letters), but also semantic (understanding by making sense from the context of the story and from the illustrations used) as well as syntactic (understanding from the context of the sentence structure). These are referred to as "cueing systems" (Adams, 1998) and should be explicitly taught to children to use as aids in their learning. By supporting children's use of these strategies, providing exposure and guidance matched to their stage of development, and encouraging children by accepting their reading efforts without emphasizing errors, teachers and the adults in their lives will be setting the stage for optimal literacy progress.

WRITING DEVELOPMENT

While writing development generally emerges in predictable stages, no one can predict how long a child will take to master each one. The stages of writing begin with marks and scribbles, progressing to letter writing, phonetic spelling, and the use of conventional words and symbols.

Making Marks

A child's first attempt at writing is generally scribble-like marks that seem to go in every direction. These usually include large circular marks that are uncontrolled and resemble drawing (National Association for the Education of Young Children, 1998).

Figure 12.1. Early Stage of Writing

While the marks do not typically resemble print, they do represent ideas. Although the random scribbles may seem meaningless to adults, they are the foundation of all writing and signal that a child has begun the process of learning to write (Teale & Sulzby, 1986).

In the early stages of writing development, there is often not much difference between a child's writing and his or her drawing. Children at this stage will often "draw" letters just as they draw pictures of objects. As conventional writing begins to develop, distinctions between writing and drawing become more noticeable.

Name-Writing and Letters

Their own name is usually one of the first recognizable words children write. They also copy print they see in the environment around them. Soon, children begin to use the letters of their own name to write lists, create signs, or jot down pretend phone messages. At this stage, they are able to identify the letters of their own name in other places, such as street signs or advertisements. They also begin to understand that_different combinations of letters have specific meanings.

Figure 12.2. Name-Writing

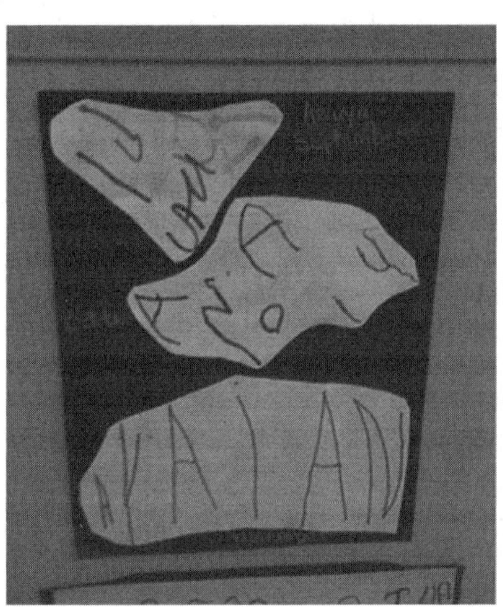

Word Writing—Phonetic Spelling

As children learn that print has meaning and become aware of different sounds, they begin to experiment with writing words phonetically. Using familiar letters and sounds, they create new words, beginning with a letter of the initial sound to represent the word, then move on to a word that is represented by the first and last sound, and finally adding the middle letters that represent the vowels and other consonants (Gentry, 1987). Teachers (and family members) can help this process by helping young children match the letters to sounds.

Figure 12.3. Phonetic Spelling

Word Writing—Conventional Spelling

The more children practice writing, the more they are read to, and the more they are surrounded by print, the more experiences they have using text, and the more they begin to use conventional spelling in their writing. Writing moves from a mix of phonetic and conventional writing to mostly conventional words. Children learn to write from left to right and top to bottom of a page, they learn to make spaces between words, they learn punctuation, they begin to string words together to make sentences, and soon they are writing stories and other genres of print.

Figure 12.4. Conventional Spelling

BALANCING EXPLICIT INSTRUCTION WITH INTENTIONAL GUIDANCE AND INDEPENDENT PLAY-BASED ACTIVITIES

The important skills of the stages of literacy development discussed previously do not happen on their own. They take place through a combination of explicit instruction, intentional guidance during active learning experiences, and children's independent explorations during play-based activities. All three types of activities are important. Learning through intentional guidance during active learning and learning through independent explorations during play-based activities have been discussed in Chapters 5 and 6. Following are more details about how explicit instruction in literacy can take place through a Balanced Literacy program (Fountas & Pinnell, 2001).

Balanced Literacy

Balanced Literacy is implemented through a "Reading and Writing Workshop Model" (Calkins, 1994, 2000). Its overall purpose is to provide differentiated instruction that will support the reading and writing skill development of each individual. The teacher begins by modeling the reading/writing strategy that is the focus of the workshop during a mini-lesson. Then, children read leveled texts (selected to be "just right" for the stage of development they have attained in their reading) independently or write independently for an extended period of time as the teacher circulates among them to observe, record observations, and confer. At the culmination of the workshop session, selected children share their strategies and their work with the class.

The following are components of Balanced Literacy:

Read-Aloud. Read-aloud is a time where the teacher reads aloud to a group of children. This experience builds print awareness; models reading behaviors (such as handling a book and reading from top to bottom and left to right); develops phonological and phonemic awareness; models fluent and expressive reading; develops listening and reading comprehension skills by asking questions and leading discussions about books before, during, and after reading; exposes children to new vocabulary; and helps children recognize what reading for pleasure is all about. Reading aloud is arguably one of the most important things parents and teachers can do with children.

Shared Reading. Shared reading is an interactive reading experience that involves children sharing the reading of a book or other text while guided and supported by a teacher. The teacher explicitly models the skills of proficient readers, including reading with fluency and expression. The type of texts used in shared reading varies by grade level, but typically in the kindergarten through 2nd grades, students read one enlarged text, such as a Big Book perched on an easel or the edge of the chalkboard, a poem or chant copied onto chart paper and hanging on a chart stand or the blackboard, class sets of picture books, or a short text copied onto a transparency and projected on the overhead. During the reading, the teacher uses a pointer or hand to track the print as it is read. Shared reading helps to build book and print awareness in kindergarten and 1st-grade students by modeling reading behaviors, such as reading from top to bottom and left to right; it builds phonics skills in students by providing instruction and repeated practice in decoding books on their independent level; and it increases the reading accuracy and fluency of students by providing instruction and repeated practice in reading a text quickly, easily, and with expression.

Reading Workshop. During a reading workshop, skills are explicitly modeled during mini-lessons. The mini-lesson has four parts—the connection, the teach (demonstration), the active engagement, and the link. The teacher chooses a skill and strategy that she believes her class needs based on assessments she has conducted in her classroom. During the connection, she connects prior learning to the current skill she is teaching that day. She then states the teaching point or the skill and strategy she is going to teach. She then shows students how to do the skill by modeling the strategy in a book with which they are familiar. She often uses a "think-aloud" to show students what she is thinking. Students then try the work out in their own books or in the teacher's book during the active engagement. During the link, she reminds students of all the strategies they can do while they are independently reading.

Independent Reading. Independent reading is a time for children to read texts that are of interest to them on their own—books, magazines, or newspapers—with minimal to no assistance from adults.

Guided Reading. Guided reading is a time—usually during independent reading—when teachers work with small groups of children to practice using decoding and comprehension strategies as they read a text that is on their instructional level (which means they can read it with about 90% accuracy). The teacher works with a small group to support their reading, making decisions about group membership and the focus of the lesson based upon ongoing assessment of where children are on the continuum of literacy development. Teachers make sure to pick a text that is on the appropriate level and that allows children to practice a strategy that will address a pre-identified need. Guided reading serves several purposes: It builds book and print awareness in early readers, it develops phonics skills, it supports children to develop reading accuracy and fluency, and it helps to develop reading comprehension skills. Some of the comprehension strategies children are taught include sequencing, relating background knowledge, making inferences, comparing and contrasting, summarizing, synthesizing, problem solving, distinguishing between fact and opinion, finding the main idea, and supporting details.

Word Study. Word study is a time for learning word patterns, word recognition, vocabulary, and phonics, as well as spelling (Rasinski & Zutell, 2010). This can take place in literacy centers or during group time.

Writing Workshop. Writing workshop functions in much the same way as reading workshop. Children are explicitly taught skills and strategies for writing during a mini-lesson. Then they go off and write independently—either about an assigned topic or whatever they choose—to use the skills presented that day. The teacher comes around and confers with students to help them with their goals (Atwell, 1989). The workshop usually ends with individuals sharing their work with the class.

Throughout the process of writing workshop, children progress from generating ideas to planning/rehearsing, to drafting, to revising, to editing, to publishing and celebrating. Throughout the process of both reading and writing workshops, children progress from having teacher support to being independent learners—acquiring the strategies needed to understand texts by themselves and to write independently.

PROVIDING SUPPORTS FOR CHILDREN'S VARIED DEVELOPMENT

Through all the different kinds of learning experiences that are needed in classrooms for young children—described here in terms of literacy—it is important to remember that although children in a grade may all be the same age, they are not necessarily in the same place in their development. Development of young children is varied—both *when* children develop certain skills and in *what order* they develop different skills. One child may be advanced in literacy but not as developed in mathematical understandings. Another may have physical prowess beyond others her age but be at earlier stages of reading and writing. Another may be learning in a language that is different from the one spoken at his home. The fact that standards have been articulated by grades makes it problematic for teachers and schools to nurture this naturally uneven development. However, if educators can be both mindful of external expectations and work to build on individual children's strengths, interests, and the home languages in which they have grown up, chances are enhanced that forward progress will be made for a range of different kinds of learners.

CHAPTER 13

Teaching Strategies to Support Children's Learning

> Perhaps the most difficult thing to get is intellectual sympathy and intellectual insight that will enable one to provide the conditions for another person's thinking and yet allow that other person to do his thinking in his own way and not according to some scheme which we have prepared in advance. This applies quite as much to the teaching of the elementary school subjects, such as arithmetic and grammar, as to the reflections of the adult discoverer. At present, we often think that a child has no right to solve a problem or do a sum at all unless he goes through a certain form.
>
> —John Dewey, 1914

When thinking about what we teach and how we teach it, the continued theme of this text is that our actions need to be grounded in our purposes. We need to be constantly mindful of what it is that we want learners to come to understand as a result of our time with them in school. Our goals then should inform our teaching practices, our curriculum patterns, and even our organizational structures and relationships with students and families (Perrone, 1991).

PURPOSES GUIDE TEACHING

As we think about purposes, we need to consider such questions as those posed by Vito Perrone (1991): Do we want children to know the mechanics of reading but not develop a love for reading? Do we want children to perform math computation but not understand what the computations mean? Do we want children to be obedient followers of rules but not know how to construct rules and guidelines for themselves and their communities to address our human problems and challenges?

If we agree with Jean Piaget, the developmental theorist and scientist, that the goal of education should be to support the creation of creative and critical thinkers (Piaget in Greene, 1978), then we need to hone teaching practices that support these goals. And if we agree with John Dewey's view, now validated by neuroscience, that young children are always learning—that is their nature (Dewey, 1938; Shonkoff & Phillips, 2000)—then we also need to find ways to make schools fit the nature of the child, rather than to insist that the child fit the school. We need to aim for teaching that supports children's understandings, that nurtures their critical faculties, that feeds their creativity and imagination, that supports them to be caring and compassionate members of our human community. We need to provide opportunities for them to construct their own understandings of the complexities of our world rather than have them just passively learn about knowledge that was developed by others. We need to help them make connections between ideas and their own understandings. We need to help them experience and practice democracy rather than just read about it as a distant phenomenon (Darling-Hammond, 1997, 2008, 2010, 2015; Dewey, 1916).

To achieve these goals, we want to help children develop capacities to persevere, manage their feelings, listen with understanding and empathy, question and pose problems, investigate solutions to these problems, apply past understandings to new situations, take risks, be reflective, think flexibly and independently, communicate with clarity and precision, strive for accuracy, create, imagine, innovate, remain open to continuous learning, and be able to see the wonderment and awe in the world (Costa & Kallick, 2009).

TEACHING STRATEGIES TO MATCH PURPOSES

A variety of teaching strategies match these purposes. One is providing children with multiple opportunities to explore, create, and get immersed in real-life experiences. David Hawkins (1965) called this "messing about"—an initial stage of working with almost any material before asking children to engage in teacher-directed activities with materials.

Other teaching strategies to support the development of children's deep thinking are for teachers to do the following: demonstrate possibilities for discovery and exploration (in whole and small groups); communicate high expectations and respect—for children in general and for their ideas; give children responsibility for the care of the materials they use; provide opportunities to practice new skills and to experiment with unfamiliar materials; invite children to experiment and come up with their own solutions to problems; support children to make decisions and guide their own investigations; and interact with children by asking questions, reflecting back to them what they know, and offering educative/constructive feedback on their work and ideas (Cambourne, 2002).

Asking Educative Questions

An effective way to stay true to the purposes discussed previously is to stay away from primary reliance on teaching as telling and, instead, provide ample opportunities for children to actively engage in self-directed activities and experiences. As we interact with them in these experiences, and in other activities such as meetings and lessons, we want to be mindful of the kinds of questions we ask. We want to steer away from only asking questions that have a predetermined answer or that have answers of only yes/no, right/wrong, or true/false. Rather, we want to offer children questions that are more open-ended—that is, questions that stimulate their thinking and guide them to where and/or how answers can be found (Harlen, 1985). These kinds of questions often begin with words such as "what," "how," "who," or "why."

Following are some examples of such educative questions, discussed in order of their level of complexity, that guide children to think, explore, and discover.

Attention-Focusing Questions. The most basic kind of question when exploring an issue is an attention-focusing question that can be asked to help children learn to observe. This kind of question takes the form of "What do you notice?" "What happened?" "What do you find inside?" "What do you hear?" These kinds of questions guide children's observations and lead them to take note of what they may not have previously seen.

Basic Noticing Questions. An extension of this basic question is a basic noticing question, which is more specific: For example, a question about measuring and counting. Examples of such questions are, "How many?" "How long?" "How often?"

Comparison Questions. Basic observational questions can lead to comparison questions, which are more cognitively complex, aimed at getting the learner to think about differences and make sharper observations. Examples are, "Is it longer, stronger, heavier?" "In how many ways are your seeds alike and different (shape, color, size, texture, structure, markings, etc.)?" Questions like these help learners make order and classify things in the world. Activities that support this kind of skill are playing classifying games, using attribute blocks, and making charts and tables.

Action Questions. Action questions are another kind of question that take basic noticing ideas and extend them into what can be done with what is noticed. "What happens if?" is an action question that can be asked during simple explorations. "What happens if you put a plant cutting in water?" "What happens when you put a magnet near metal?"

"What happens when you put lettuce in the guinea pig cage?" "What happens when you cut into a pumpkin?" These kinds of questions help children discover the relationship between what they do and what happens as a consequence of their actions.

To get the most out of such questions, however, children need to have prior opportunities for open-ended exploration, which will help them learn what possibilities and impossibilities there are and become familiar with the properties of the subjects they are studying. These opportunities for open-ended exploration before any questioning will better equip children to engage in problem solving and "what happens if" questions afterward.

Another action question—a prediction question—can be posed to get them thinking: "What do you think will happen if . . . ?" or "Can you find a way?" These particular questions set up possibilities for real problem-solving situations in which learners will be challenged to recognize variables and engage in more sophisticated study.

How and Why Questions. Only after lots of experiences and after all of the preceding kinds of questions have been offered should teachers try to ask how and why questions and reasoning questions that call for children to provide some sort of explanation. Even then, teachers should use these kinds of questions with caution because they can easily lead to asking for the "right" answer and the teacher "telling," rather than having children rely on their experiences to make conjectures. To genuinely support understanding, we want to get children to think and reason based on their own experiences, not what someone has told them. We want them to reflect on their experiences, draw relationships, and make generalizations. And when we finally ask how and why questions, we want to make sure that we open up discussion and invite children to freely express what and how they think about their observations and findings. Discussion, dialogue, and sharing of ideas help children to recognize new relationships and develop their understandings. To provide an atmosphere that is conducive to these conversations, we need to make sure that children feel safe to talk freely and to not be afraid of making a "mistake," as "mistakes" reveal a lot about what they understand and what they think. When Yvonne's class, in Chapter 9, discussed their observations of the rotting carved pumpkin, they began with what they noticed, moved on to comparing the difference between the rotting carved pumpkin and the intact uncarved pumpkin, and then finally entertained questions about why the carved pumpkin rotted and why the intact pumpkin didn't. Each child's response, whether inaccurate or factual, was met with respectful consideration.

One way to phrase a why question that conveys respect for a child's thinking even if it is factually inaccurate is to ask, "Why, do you think?" (Harlen, Darwin, & Murphy, 1977). Framing the question in this way indicates that rather than seeking the "right answer," you are trying to understand the child's thinking in order to help the child move forward to make sense of the situation.

Another kind of how and why question that requires care in responding is the how/why question that is asked by children themselves. Teachers should approach such children's questions by, whenever possible, offering opportunities to figure it out. Sometimes when children ask why, the teacher may not know the answer. In this case, the teacher can guide children to research in books or to seek out an "expert" who may be able to help. Sometimes the answer to the question may not yet be known. Or sometimes the question can lead to explorations in other fields, which may lead to philosophical contemplations that may be beyond their comprehension. Regardless, the important thing is to help children understand that questions generally lead to more questions and that others grapple with questions at all stages of their development and throughout their entire lives.

Nurturing Children's Own Questions

Powerful learning is nurtured when children are given ample opportunities to frame their own questions as a result of open-ended experiences and activities linked to appropriate questions from the teacher (Elstgeest, 1985). Providing an extended period of choice time when children can work in centers and engage in child-initiated activities with materials is a way to encourage questions that are rich with possibilities for learning.

Teachers can use whole-group class time to encourage children's inquiries, such as, for example, the question of "Do flamingos fly?" raised by children in Fanny Roman's class in Chapter 6. This question led to the class's study of birds, which then led to the question of "What else flies?," which led to the class's aviation study. Children can be invited to discuss such interesting questions, the things they have observed, and the questions that have arisen in morning meetings, read-alouds, and choice time reflections. Group meetings can also be a time to set up a routine of "questions of the week" or to make charts that keep track of their questions or wonderings on a theme or study in which the whole class is involved (see Figure 6.2).

Another strategy for supporting children's thinking and learning is to establish procedures by which children are encouraged to reflect on some work in which they are engaged—either individually or collectively—and keep track of these on lists or charts or in journals. The choice-time reflection journals used in Fanny's kindergarten classroom (see Chapter 6) and the charts used in Emma's prekindergarten classroom (in Chapter 8) documenting what they know about trains (see Figure 8.3) are good examples of this kind of reflection.

Setting Up the Environment to Facilitate Children's Questions

The entire atmosphere of the classroom can be thoughtfully set up to enhance children's learning and nurture children's questions. Teachers can add questions to displays and collections set up in the science corner. They can work with children to create lists of questions to investigate. They can make sure any work cards or worksheets placed in the different centers of the classroom are framed in terms of investigable questions. Remember: Familiar as well as novel materials are rich with possibilities for questions.

Perhaps the most powerful thing that teachers can do to establish a culture of inquiry in the class is to model good question-asking skills ourselves. Children learn from what we do. If we show them how we ourselves reflect and wonder and pursue questions, our learners will gain images of how to reflect and wonder and question themselves, and begin to do this in a similar manner.

CHAPTER 14

Celebrating Diversity

No way. The hundred is there.
The child is made of one hundred.
The child has a hundred languages
a hundred hands
a hundred thoughts
a hundred ways of thinking
of playing,
of speaking.
A hundred
always a hundred ways of listening
of marveling, of loving
a hundred joys for singing and understanding
a hundred worlds to discover
a hundred worlds to invent
a hundred worlds to dream.

—Loris Malaguzzi, "No way. The hundred is there."
(in Edwards, Gandini, & Forman, 1998, p. 3)

Earlier chapters have discussed a variety of strategies for supporting children's learning. While important and necessary, these are not sufficient. If we are to realize high-quality learning for *all* children, teaching strategies need to always be responsive to, relevant to, and sustaining of children's different cultures, languages, family backgrounds, and differing strengths and needs. Toward the beginning of this book the importance of getting to know the children, families, cultures, and communities represented in any class was discussed. A critical next step is to ensure that this information is used to craft teaching strategies and supports that are sustaining, responsive, and relevant to this diversity. Culturally responsive, relevant, and sustaining teaching includes the following: viewing children's and families' cultural and linguistic heritages as assets and funds of knowledge for teaching (Gonzalez, Moll, & Amanti, 2005; Moll et al., 1992; Purcell-Gates, 2007); believing that all children can learn and supporting them to experience a sense of self-worth and a trust in their abilities; valuing differences and varied ways of learning; recognizing language development as diverse and supporting each child's unique trajectory; working to eliminate power imbalances in the classroom based on differences; and supporting children to recognize, interrogate, challenge, and transform inequities, injustices, oppressions, exploitations, power, and privilege (Au & Jordan, 1981; Ballenger, 1998; Banks, 2006; García & Frede, 2010; García, Lin, & May, 2017; Gay, 2002, 2010, 2013; Gonzalez et al., 2005; Irvine, 2003; Ladson-Billings, 1994, 1995, 2005, 2006; Souto-Manning et al., 2018).

RECOGNIZING CHILDREN'S AND FAMILIES' CULTURES AND COMMUNITIES AS VALUABLE RESOURCES FOR LEARNING

Key to being a responsive educator is to find the strengths each child brings to the learning enterprise and the "funds of knowledge" (Gonzalez et al., 2005; Moll et al., 1992; Purcell-Gates, 2007) and cultural assets possessed by children's families and communities (Paris & Alim, 2017). Framing children's and families' differences as assets rather than deficits and recognizing, valuing, and including them in the work of school are critical supports for children's optimal development.

Valuing and partnering with learners and their families to honor differences involves using knowledge of children's diverse languages and cultures, families, and communities to guide curriculum development, classroom climates, instructional strategies, and relationships with students. This is done by incorporating the children's cultures and languages in all subjects and skills that are taught and by representing various ethnic and cultural groups in the context of academics, processes, and skills. Additionally, culturally responsive/relevant/sustaining teachers teach to and through children's personal and cultural strengths, their intellectual capabilities, and their prior accomplishments. Ways to do this include using materials and displays that children can relate to culturally and linguistically, such as items from their homes, photos of their families and neighborhoods, and their music, activities, food, and traditions. Materials that have direct connection to the children, families, and communities are generally more effective than commercially produced products. For example, when studying "the community," a book created by a teacher and children that uses photos of their actual neighborhood is more relatable than a purchased book with illustrations of generic community helpers. When studying families, real food packages that families have on their shelves at home are more relevant to place in the dramatic play area than purchased "pretend" foods. Additionally, discussions—whether about history or issues—reflect the perspectives of all who are or were involved, not just those of the dominant culture (i.e., indigenous peoples' views of Thanksgiving; the varied configurations of what makes a family, etc.).

Partnering with families to enrich the curriculum is also a key element of culturally responsive/relevant/sustaining teaching. Family members can be enlisted to participate during the school day as resources for storytelling, cooking, explaining and celebrating holidays and traditions, and leading other culturally and linguistically meaningful activities. By filtering curriculum and teaching strategies through the cultural frames of reference of the learners and their families, culturally responsive teaching makes learning more personally meaningful, easier to master, and more accurately related to the lived realities of our diverse world (see Figures 2.16–2.17).

In these ways, culturally responsive/relevant/sustaining teaching aims to replace deficit perceptions—of children, communities of color, and others who are marginalized or minoritized—with positive ones. By recognizing the potential, creativity, imagination, ingenuity, resourcefulness, accomplishments, and resilience that individuals and families possess, this approach to teaching aspires to create constructive, sustainable learning experiences. In doing so, this teaching counters the negativism that traps children and their families in assumptions of marginality and disadvantage. It also aims to offset teachers' attitudes and actions that range from not caring about or being uncomfortable with relating to diverse students and families; to teachers thinking they do not have the knowledge, skills, and dispositions to teach those who are not in the mainstream; to teachers who actually hold prejudiced views. This kind of teaching celebrates differences.

BELIEVING THAT ALL CHILDREN CAN LEARN

In addition to honoring and infusing children's cultures and realities into the learning life of the classroom, culturally responsive/relevant/sustaining teachers validate, facilitate, and empower diverse learners to be successful out of a belief that all children can learn. They do this by building on learners' strengths and cultural backgrounds, as described previously. And they use this pathway through children's strengths to make sure that all the children in their class are supported to develop the skills and knowledge—reading, writing, content knowledge—of the dominant "culture of power" (Delpit, 1988). Doing this cultivates cooperation, collaboration, reciprocity, and mutual respect among and between learners.

A culturally responsive/relevant/sustaining teacher also ensures that the curriculum and the teaching that takes place in the classroom are challenging for and supportive of all children. This means that everyone has access to opportunities for enrichment, for creative and critical thinking, and to engage in higher-order thinking. Opportunities for learning are equally distributed, regardless of age, size, or so-called ability. While placing children in groups according to their needs in regard to the development of specific skills can be helpful at times, the groups are fluid and do not limit children from being exposed to the same challenging content of ideas to which children who are more advanced along the skill-development continuum are exposed. This means that a child who is at an early stage in reading could be in a guided reading group with others who are at that same early stage in reading (Fountas & Pinnell, 2016), but at the same time the child may be more developed in math and thus placed in a math group with children who are advanced in their math skills and understandings. This also means that all children, no matter where they are in the continuum of progress in their mathematics or literacy skills, have opportunities to share in the same rich discussions, experiments, projects, and experiences about ideas and issues that take place in the class during meetings and project/center/inquiry time.

Another indicator of culturally responsive/relevant/sustaining teachers who believe that all children can learn is that they assume responsibility for the progress of children's learning. If a child doesn't understand, the teacher takes responsibility for making sure to find another way to support that child's progress, rather than blaming the child for "just not getting it" and placing the blame on the child's lack of ability, home situation, or failure to try. Every effort is made to access multiple resources to make certain that every child gets what is needed to move forward in her or his learning.

RESPECTING VARIATION IN CHILDREN'S DEVELOPMENT

A responsive educator acknowledges, values, and supports the reality that variation in children's development is the norm, not something problematic. Variation appears in many ways: in children's pace, trajectory, and style of learning; in their different paces of emotional and social development; in their strengths, needs, and interests; in the ways they express what they know and can do; and in how their sociocultural contexts impact their learning processes.

Responsiveness to these differences is exhibited in the ways in which the day is scheduled and the physical context of the classroom is created so that children do not always have to do the same thing at the same time. Rather, they are given time and space to work on a variety of different things in different ways. A range of materials are provided, and opportunities are made available for children to interact with the materials in their own ways.

For example, choice is scheduled into the day so that children can select what they want to work on and engage in that work in whatever way they are able. The teacher is available to provide feedback that is differentiated to each child's needs. Additionally, even when all children may be engaged in the same work—such as writing workshop—different children may be producing work at different developmental levels. Again, the teacher accepts where each child is at, scaffolding instruction and providing feedback that is differentiated to the needs of each child.

Responsiveness to children's differences is also evident in the ways that teachers interact with children—they provide supports and encouragement for children to positively interact with one another. And, as noted in the previous discussion, responsiveness is also evident when teachers look for, acknowledge, and build on the strengths of each child. Strengths are supported and used strategically to address each child's vulnerabilities and needs. So, for example, for a child who struggles with reading but has special skills in art, the teacher may seek out books that have compelling illustrations. Or, for a child who is fascinated by construction vehicles or very interested in sports, the teacher could provide books and writing opportunities in these areas to utilize the child's interests as a motivator for working on literacy development.

SUPPORTING VARIATION IN CHILDREN'S LANGUAGE DEVELOPMENT

Language development in young children is also varied—it is a diverse, nonlinear, and dynamic process (Byers-Heinlein & Lew-Williams, 2013; Cummins, 2001). Research shows that young children are especially receptive to learning languages, and that language growth is directly related to the quantity and quality of speech they hear in each language they are exposed to (Ramirez & Kuhl, 2017). A responsive teacher thus recognizes, values, and supports the language development process by building on children's existing language practices and by being flexible with language in the classroom. This means that multiple languages are honored and leveraged as resources, using "translanguaging" strategies (multiple nonverbal resources such as symbols, signs, and actions) (García & Wei, 2014). Efforts are made to include, communicate with, and learn from the children, as well as with and from their families.

There are no one-size-fits-all strategies for how to support young language learners—each one is an individual. So it is up to the teacher to use information from families and observations of children in the classroom to individualize instruction. Here are some things to find out that can help determine effective strategies:

- What is the child's language background? Does she or he speak one, two, or more languages?
- What exposure to English has the child had, and in what environments?
- Is the child learning two languages at the same time? Or has the child learned a home language first, followed by a second language?
- What are the child's individual characteristics, interests, and experiences?

Based on this information, teachers—regardless of the language they speak—can provide support and encouragement to help children move forward in learning their home language as well as English. They can then use what they know to find books in the languages represented in the classroom, make classroom signs in those languages, and use translanguaging strategies wherever possible to support learning.

SUPPORTING YOUNG CHILDREN TO BE CRITICAL THINKERS

Responsive teaching requires teachers to be critical thinkers who also support learners to be critical thinkers. Culturally responsive/relevant/sustaining teachers thus include among their teaching approaches those that promote and foster questioning and problem solving. Responsive teachers are intentional in supporting young learners to gain the skills needed to interrogate social norms, stereotypes, and controversies. They make space in the classroom to problematize social inequities and to nurture children's abilities to see and respect multiple perspectives. Fairness and inclusivity are welcomed, fostered, and incorporated into classroom practices. In these ways, teachers are preparing young children to be active citizens in a democracy. As noted educator Linda Darling-Hammond has suggested: "A democratic education means that we educate people in a way that ensures they can think independently, that they can use information, knowledge, and technology, among other things, to draw their own conclusions" (retrieved from www.azquotes.com/quote/900232).

Some examples of how this is done can be found in a kindergarten classroom's study of different types of hair; a 1st-grade study of water that includes an investigation of how, in 2017, drinking water in Flint, Michigan, got polluted and what subsequent actions were taken in support of the city's citizens; and a 2nd-grade study of skin color based on a poem, followed by the creation of a mural portraying the beautiful mosaic of color that made up the group (see Figure 14.1).

Figure 14.1. Skin Colors

Even children as young as prekindergarteners can question and interrogate norms. Recycling food waste, discussing current news (such as "taking the knee" to protest racial discrimination), engaging in acts of kindness to elders or others who might be neglected, sharing differences in family structures, and having conversations about the world—its differences, prejudices, and inequities—can be a rich source of learning for children of all ages.

Figure 14.2. Antiracism Poster

REPLACING OBSTACLES WITH OPPORTUNITIES TO SUCCEED

Through all of the ways in which teaching is reframed, repositioned, and conducted that have been described in this chapter, culturally responsive/relevant/sustaining teaching aims to replace the current view of students who represent diversity as one of weakness, problems, and deficits with an orientation toward strength, promise, and possibility. By focusing and building on different learners' strengths and resiliencies, culturally responsive teaching reframes what many refer to as the "achievement gap," used to characterize disparities in the school-based achievement of learners from minoritized backgrounds, to a perspective and approach that focus on providing opportunities to those who have been the recipients of a historic "opportunity gap" (Ladson-Billings, 2006).

This approach conceptualizes replacing obstacles with opportunities to succeed. It grounds teaching in the notions that

> success generates success, that competence builds confidence, and that regardless of how marginalized or disadvantaged an individual student or ethnic group may be according to external criteria . . . , there is some kind of capability within. A key mandate of culturally responsive teaching is accessing this internal strength of ethnically diverse students and communities, and using it to improve their personal agency and educational achievement. (Gay, 2013, p. 68)

Building Community in the Classroom

Caring for the Whole Child

If children live with encouragement
They learn to be confident
If children live with praise
They learn to be appreciative
If children live with shame
They learn to feel guilty
If children live with approval
They learn to like themselves
If children live with criticism
They learn to condemn
If children live with acceptance
They learn to find love in the world
If children live with hostility
They learn to fight
If children live with recognition
They learn to have a goal
If children live with sharing
They learn to be generous
If children live with honesty and fairness
They learn what truth and justice are
If children live with security
They learn to have faith in themselves and in those around them
If children live with friendliness
They learn that the world is a nice place in which to live

—Dorothy Law Nolte, "Children Learn What They Live," 1972

As has been presented in the teaching cases in this text—all intended to represent well-organized, richly provisioned classrooms that offer interesting and meaningful real-world experiences—high-quality teaching is responsive to the individual and to the cultural and linguistic diversity in the classroom. It supports learners to progress toward mastery of critical skills and knowledge, to develop in-depth understanding, to make connections between ideas, and to assume a critical stance toward learning. This kind of curriculum "teaches the way children learn" (Falk, 2008).

Another critical element of a classroom that teaches the way children learn is a strong sense of community. A strong sense of community is achieved by using all aspects of classroom and school life as educative opportunities. These include daily routines (such as lunch and recess), the transitions that take place between one activity and another, and the interactions children have with one another (individually and in groups). This chapter discusses these elements of teaching that are generally considered to be non-academic but are nonetheless vital to the children's learning lives—what is referred to here as "a curriculum of care."

CARE NURTURES HEALTHY DEVELOPMENT

A curriculum of care acknowledges that the quality of the relationships individuals have with each other—the way minute-by-minute interactions are affected by the tone of a voice; the choice of a person's words, facial expressions, or other body language; and whether a sense of respect, caring, and generosity are conveyed—play an important role in learning. Now there is research from neuroscience to confirm this (Bransford, Brown, & Cocking, 2000; Center on the Developing Child, 2017; Lally & Mangione, 2017; Shonkoff, 2017; Shonkoff & Phillips, 2000; Siegel, 2001).

Neuroscientific Findings Confirm the Importance of Relationships

Neuroscientific findings confirm what educators and researchers of young children have long theorized—that young children's early relationships and life experiences shape later development and mental health. Science tells us that children's early experiences in life and in relationships affect the architecture of the developing brain and all future learning. What children experience in their early years impacts their executive function and self-regulation abilities, their resilience, and the emotional development that affects cognitive development.

Self-Regulation. Executive function and self-regulation skills are the mental processes that enable us to plan, focus attention, remember instructions, and exercise self-control (Bodrova & Leong, 2007). These skills enable positive behavior, allow us to make healthy choices, and are crucial for learning and development.

Resilience. Enabling self-regulation is resilience—the ability to cope with adversity such as neglect, abuse, and/or violence, all of which are toxic stressors that literally disrupt and impair brain architecture. Resilience develops as a result of protective experiences, the single most common one being a stable and committed relationship with a supportive parent, caregiver, or other adult. This kind of relationship can buffer children from stressors that can be disruptive to development (Pakulak et al., 2017; Shonkoff, 2017). It can mobilize sources of hope, faith, and cultural traditions and also help to foster a sense of self-efficacy by providing guidance and a personalized responsiveness that nurtures self-regulation and adaptive skill-building.

While children are not born with executive function, self-regulation, and resilience skills, they *are* born with the potential to develop them. So providing the support that children need to build these skills is one of the most important responsibilities of early childhood caregivers and teachers. Activities that foster this process are creative play, exercise, and social connections. These help children direct their own actions, cope with stress, and practice needed life skills before they must perform them alone. Adults nurture the development of these abilities by establishing routines, modeling behavior, and creating and maintaining supportive, reliable relationships. Adults also support these skills by engaging in what neuroscientists refer to as "serve and return" (Shonkoff, 2017; Shonkoff et al., 2012).

Serve and Return. Serve and return refers to the back-and-forth between a child and a meaningful adult that creates emotional bonds. The exchange is about noticing and responding to a child's focus of attention—a sound, a facial expression, a movement. It also involves reflecting back and naming to a child what she has said, done, and/or understood. This back-and-forth between caregiver and child makes important language connections in the child's brain, even if the child cannot yet talk. It signals to the child that her thoughts and feelings are heard and understood, lets the child know that she is cared for, and helps the child understand the world, know what to expect, and develop new vocabulary. Serve-and-return interactions also help children learn self-control and how to get along with others, while providing the responsive adult with information about the child's abilities, interests, and needs.

When adults are responsive to children and acknowledge and address children's questions, concerns, understandings, and interests, they help to build children's skills for facing life's challenges. This sets the foundation for children's lifelong learning, behavior, and health.

DISCIPLINING THROUGH A COMMUNITY-OF-CARE APPROACH

The philosopher Nel Noddings (1984, 2013) conceptualizes caring as the development of enduring, reciprocal, and responsive relationships. She theorizes that teachers can teach care through modeling, practice, dialogue, confirmation, and, most of all, knowing students well. An ethic of care needs to be at the center of all educational practices.

Children need to be in caring communities to develop the sense of self-worth necessary to take the risks involved in genuine learning. In the same way that they need explicit attention to skills and content knowledge in meaningful contexts to effectively learn academics, children also need explicit support for their social and emotional development by being in a context of safety, trust, and care (Copple & Bredekamp, 2009; Raver, 2002; Viadero, 2007).

One part of supporting children's resilience, self-regulation, and executive function skills is modeling communication strategies that offer positive approaches to managing feelings and behavior. This involves using words and a tone of voice that enable children to be involved in learning and social contexts in an engaged, active way.

Using Educative Language to Support Positive Behavior

To guide children toward choosing and maintaining positive behaviors, adults need to choose their words and tone of voice carefully and strategically in order to consciously use language in an educative way. For example, when responding to children's problematic behaviors, rather than berating or blaming, an educative approach would be to comment in ways that help children understand what they have done that is helpful, or what can be done to change what is unacceptable. "Does anyone know why I might be stopping the whole class from reading? It is too loud in here for everyone to be able to do their best reading. Quiet please." Or, "You know what? People are saying really important things but they don't get heard because people aren't listening to each other. It is José's turn to speak now. Let's show respect to José by giving him our full attention."

Comments like these give guidance to children for how to achieve the cooperative atmosphere teachers want to establish. This kind of atmosphere is one that helps children think about others as well as themselves.

Not only words, but also tone of voice, facial expressions, and body posture communicate messages. It is important to coordinate these to convey respect and support. Avoid shaming, using sarcasm, or getting into power struggles. Use direct and clear language. Keep the focus on the positive behavior you want to encourage. Here is an example: Tell children directly what to do ("Finish up what you are working on, please, then put your materials away and join me in the meeting area") instead of pitting the children who are following directions against those who are not ("Nita is following the rules; why can't the rest of you do that?").

Giving directions to children about what they need to do rather than asking them through a question is another strategy to guide children's behavior in an educative way. Instead of asking, "Would you please stop talking?" try stating: "Natalie has something important to say. We need to give her our full attention." Asking a question about something that in truth is nonnegotiable sets up the possibility of a confrontation. A way to avoid this and give children a sense of ownership over what they do is, whenever possible, to offer children a choice, making sure that both choices have acceptable outcomes. When teachers offer choices during the day—such as asking students to choose which of two books they would like to read or whether they would like apples or oranges for snack (please note, both of these options are acceptable to the teacher)—children develop a sense of ownership and investment. When it is not possible for teachers to give children a choice, it helps if teachers can explain why, rather than asserting their authority just because they are the teachers. For example, "You need to clean up now because it is time for us to go home."

Another way to support positive behavior through language is to describe *what* to do rather than what *not* to do. For example, a teacher can say, "Walk, please," rather than "Don't run," or "Put the blocks on the shelf when you're done" rather than "Don't leave blocks all over the floor."

One other way to provide educative feedback is to address the present ("If you are upset with her for grabbing the blocks, use a big strong voice to tell her to stop") instead of referencing history ("You are always hitting other children").

Using language like that described in these examples mirrors to children their positive actions and guides appropriate behavior. It lets them see that their positive actions are noticed and how the community of learners they are a part of benefits from their actions. "I see that you offered to help your friends clean up in the block area. That helped make the cleanup go faster." This way of communicating highlights children's strengths.

Providing feedback that helps children become aware of what they are doing is more educative than feedback that is purely evaluative—even when the feedback is positive. (Instead of saying, "Beautiful painting," try to share details of what the child did in the painting: "I see you used many different shades of blue for the sky." Or, replace "You are so good today, boys and girls" with "What a great day! Everyone listened to each other and worked together.")

Another important guideline to remember when communicating with young children is to speak to the individual's behavior and its impact rather than to the individual and her character: "When you say things like that, it hurts her feelings," instead of "You are being so mean!"

Also, try to problem-solve challenging behaviors rather than threaten punishment that is unrelated to the behavior. Instead of saying, "If you don't stop that you will get benched for recess," work with the child to figure out how he could act differently ("What could you do differently when he tries to grab your toy?").

Focus on behavior that is helpful, not on emphasizing adult approval. Instead of "I like the way you are sitting so nicely," try saying, "When you sit quietly, we can hear each other speak."

And finally, notice what is going well and use reinforcing language to comment on it. Look for positives and encouragements to say about each child, even those who have challenges and histories of difficulties. When you see a child who has caught herself from doing something, name it and reflect it back to let her know that she is making progress ("You waited your turn, even though I know it was hard for you!"). Or say to the group: "Did you notice all the helpful ideas you all gave at our meeting today?"

CREATING COMMUNITY

Empathizing with children's feelings through language is an important way to support positive behavior and establish a sense of community in the classroom. Empathizing and speaking to a child's feelings ("I know it is hard to wait, but everyone needs to have a turn") yields more positive reactions from children than criticizing behavior, which can seem to imply ill intent ("You seem to like to disrupt the meeting time"). Empathy can also be combined with language that lets all children know that they are safe while redirecting an individual's unacceptable behavior. For example, when a child is hitting in anger, a teacher may stop him or her and say, "I can see that you are very angry. But I cannot allow you to hurt Davre. I wouldn't let him do that to you or anyone else in the classroom. You need to tell Davre how you feel with words, not with hitting."

Helping children think about how their actions and words might impact others also contributes to establishing a caring community. For example, at a class meeting a teacher might say, "Use a big voice, please. This will make it easier for the listeners." Or, as children get ready to leave their classroom for a walk through the halls of the school or center, the teacher might remind them, "Remember, other children are working in their classrooms. Let's keep our voices low so that we don't disturb them." Communication strategies like these build on children's strengths rather than focus on their weaknesses. They help children see themselves in a positive light and guide them toward ways they can grow and improve.

Critical for creating a caring community is helping children to see themselves as capable individuals and responsible community members. When adults convey those assumptions and expectations to children, children are helped to build that self-perception. The words that adults choose to use with children need to convey the belief that children want to cooperate, listen, and do good work. The words adults use should also give children guidance about how they can follow through on those intentions. For example, instead of using punitive language while giving directions ("If you can't clean up the blocks, you won't be allowed to play in the block area"), try giving directions that guide children toward desired results: "Thank you for working with your friends to stack the blocks into same-size pairs and put them on the shelves. When you are done, please join the others in the meeting area."

These two ways of talking send very different messages: The first way communicates a lack of faith in the child's ability to follow the rules. It also sets up the adult as an "enforcer," undermining a sense of trust in the adult. The second way offers guidance for what to do while also communicating that the adult believes the child has good intentions, will be responsible, and, most importantly, will succeed. By using positive language in this way, adults convey belief in children's abilities and intentions, helping them to internalize a positive identity and to develop self-control.

Creating an atmosphere where everyone feels equally valued and safe develops motivation to do what is best for learning and for the group. This can be done without offering stickers, candy, or other material rewards; without singling children out in front of the class as a result of their negative *or* positive behavior; without giving coveted jobs as a reward for doing something well; without comparing children against one another; without displaying the work of only the more academically successful. Instead, order, discipline, and positive behaviors can be achieved by building on children's strengths, helping them to feel good about themselves, and trusting them to do the right thing.

Problems can be tackled by encouraging children to consult with one another and work together to figure things out rather than only relying on adults as the sole authorities who have all the answers. Such a "talking-things-through" approach can begin in the very first days of school. For example, children can generate rules for the class during a class meeting. This sends them the message that the words we use and the ways we treat one another make a difference in the quality of our lives.

Figure 15.1. Class-Generated Rules

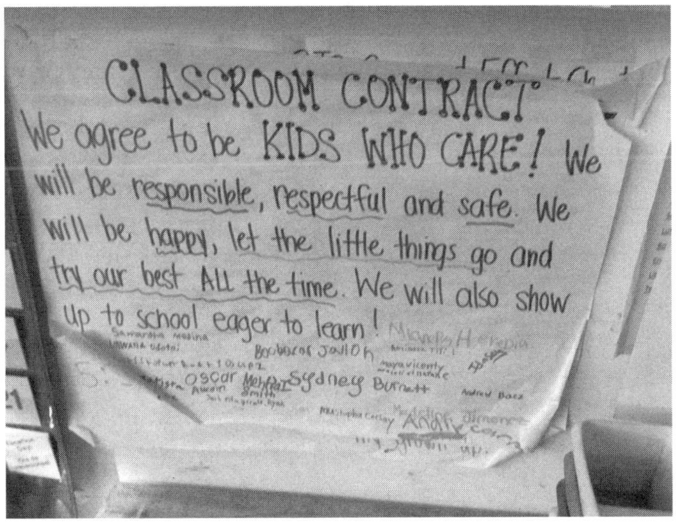

Other community-building strategies include regularly practicing mindfulness and gratefulness, developing emotionally responsive curricula (such as learning about "wants and needs," and learning to care for teddy bears), and engaging in sharing activities that invite children to listen to one another and get to know about one another's lives. These strategies are described in Chapter 16.

The actions and language of care exemplified in this chapter can do much to keep discipline problems at bay and to build a caring, democratic community in the classroom. Engaging in these practices helps children build their own inner controls, their good feelings about themselves, and their capacities to care about other people. Disciplining in this way is based on guiding rather than controlling behavior. When educators guide rather than try to control behavior, fewer infractions of the rules result, and even the majority of those problems remaining can be handled effectively through dialogue and empathic support (Kohn, 2004).

Creating an atmosphere of dialogue, democracy, and respect is not an easy task, especially because so many of us were raised and are accustomed to regulating behavior with punishments and rewards. But when old ways are broken and new norms of respect, courtesy, and nonjudgmental guidance are established, children feel accepted and loved, which, in turn, earns their cooperation and trust. Experiencing relationships in such a culture is as deep and profound a lesson in social studies as anyone could learn anywhere.

> When you plant lettuce, if it does not grow well, you don't blame the lettuce. You look for reasons it is not doing well. It may need fertilizer, or more water, or less sun. You never blame the lettuce. Yet if we have problems with our friends or family, we blame the other person. But if we know how to take care of them, they will grow well, like the lettuce. Blaming has no positive effect at all, nor does trying to persuade using reason and argument. That is my experience. No blame, no reasoning, no argument, just understanding. If you understand, and you show that you understand, you can love, and the situation will change. (Hanh, 1992)

CHAPTER 16

Creating a Caring Community of Learners in Kimberly and Vanessa's 1st/2nd-Grade Classroom

This chapter describes socially–emotionally responsive practices in a 1st/2nd-grade ICT classroom at the Earth School, a public elementary school located on the Lower East Side of New York City. Kimberly Fritschy, an experienced early childhood educator, and Vanessa Keller, an experienced special education teacher, focus on building a caring community as they team-teach this multiage group.

STRATEGIES FOR BUILDING A CARING COMMUNITY IN THE CLASSROOM

Among the strategies that Vanessa and Kimberly use are the following: introducing a 6-week initial curriculum that lays the foundation of community building, creating monthly sharing themes, teaching about wants and needs, using teddy bears to help children learn empathy, providing regular snack times, and establishing routines of mindfulness and gratitude.

Laying the Foundation of Community

Vanessa and Kimberly spend the first 6 weeks of school laying the foundation of the classroom community. During this time period, the curriculum consists of getting to know one another and establishing routines—explaining how to line up and how to clean up, introducing the cleanup song, setting expectations for the day, creating routines and rules for using the bathroom, and teaching the students how to take care of materials in the classroom. The students learn where the materials are located, how to sit in the meeting area, how to ask for help when needed, how to get to the bathroom, how to use water, how to walk through the school, and what it means to be a part of the classroom community. All of these things are important, as Vanessa explains:

> When you do it every year it can feel redundant, but if you skip it, you notice it. So, for example, we introduce one material at a time. We don't use markers until we've talked about markers. . . . And we don't use glue until we've really talked about the glue. And if you skip that, you see that the kids don't remember how to take care of things. So, it's a really slow start.

Learning to Listen and Care Through Sharing Routines

After about the first 6 weeks of school, Vanessa and Kimberly's class starts to really get to know one another. It is then that they begin their share routine, which is a structured time in which everyone has a week that they are assigned to bring something to share with the class. Each month there is a different share topic. They begin with a summer artifact—a seashell or a picture of them with their family or a drawing that they made of something that they did over the summer. And then the next share is a family artifact. Other topics of sharing might be what you did over the weekend or over the break, what your favorite food is, what your favorite color is, or a personal story. As Vanessa explains:

> A part of the sharing that we do is listening, and we really speak to the kids a lot about listening; not just being present while someone is speaking—but active listening. And we'll ask them questions to just engage them in the listening process. Building community comes from knowing each other. When you know about somebody, you're less likely to tease them and you're more likely to care for them. So I think that's why we spend so much time on that.

Learning About Wants and Needs

Early in the school year, as the children begin to share with each other about their families, the teachers introduce them to learning about the difference between "wants and needs." First, they share their own personal wants and needs with the class and then discuss the wants and needs of the classroom community. Because the classroom is an integrated general education/special education classroom, the children learn to understand that everyone in the community needs different things to get to the same place. Conversations from there lead them to creating a class charter. The teachers ask the students about how they want to feel at school and construct a long list of words in response. Then they narrow it down to a few words and create a charter, which is about making sure that everyone in the community feels "happy, included, calm, safe and loved." The entire class signs the charter, and then it is posted in the classroom. Kimberly explains: "Coming up with those emotions, those feelings of love and safety, is the heart of our social/emotional work. We wanted kids to understand their feelings and express themselves and develop empathy for their peers as well as with other people in the community" (see Figure 15.1).

Developing Empathy: The Teddy Bear Initiative

To support understandings of wants and needs—both individually and in community—every child in the class is given a teddy bear. Inspired by the work of Lesley Koplow (2002), the teachers have the children use the bears as a transitional object for themselves in coping with their own emotions. The children role-play with the bears to help them figure out how to navigate relationships with their peers. Some children build homes for their bears out of shoeboxes. Some make clothes for them. And all just generally take care of their bears. In the course of these activities, Kimberly and Vanessa invite the children to think about the bears as if they were living members of the classroom and to consider their needs and wants as well.

Structures That Support Community

After the class explores the concepts of wants and needs among themselves, they branch out to discuss the needs and wants of the neighborhood community. They begin by taking neighborhood walks and observing the different stores, services, and people who are a part of the community. A more in-depth study follows, returning to the themes that were raised in the development of their own classroom community.

A Mixed-Age Classroom. One aspect of this classroom that creates community is that it is a mixed-age (1st and 2nd grade) group. The mixed-age classroom strengthens the sense of community because it enables all the children to learn from one another. The older children tend to be leaders in the classroom and help to guide the 1st-graders—both in terms of academic work and in setting the norms and the tone of the classroom, especially at the beginning of the year, in those first 6 weeks. As Kimberly explains:

> Because the 2nd-graders already know the routines and expectations of the classroom, they really set an example for the incoming students, and it really makes that time go much quicker and much smoother. And kids benefit more from learning from their peers in that way—learning the routines from each other.

A Collaborative Classroom. In addition to the fact that the class is a mixed-age grouping, the fact that the classroom is a collaborative (general education/special education) one creates an inclusive environment where opportunities exist for children who are at different points in their learning to share and explain things to each other—whether it is an older child explaining something to a younger child or even just a younger child talking to someone and asking questions. As Vanessa states:

> When you teach someone else or you ask someone else, you are really talking it through and learning a lot more that way. In any classroom, whether it is a mixed-age classroom or a straight grade, there are so many different needs and strengths within the community. And when you have the mixed-age class, no one is standing out because of something that may be viewed as a weakness in another community. We are all a part of the same community, and the whole spectrum of learners is all in one room. I believe it helps to have everyone feel welcomed and supported and part of the community.

Snack. Snack is provided in the classroom every day. It not only addresses the children's need for "a little something" that can sustain them during the day, but it also is a time consciously set aside to sit down together for a relaxing break. Vanessa explains: "Everyone has to be really comfortable before they can learn. So, snack is a big part of that—having a break in your day so that you can sit down and eat and talk at your table." Children are encouraged to take turns passing out napkins and getting ready for snack, wait until everyone has been served to eat, make sure everyone has enough, serve one another and talk to one another, and not shout across the room while eating. It is an important time of the day that builds community and consideration for others.

Practicing Mindfulness and Gratitude

Other strategies that contribute to the sense of community in Vanessa and Kimberly's classroom are mindfulness and gratefulness.

Mindfulness. Several mindfulness techniques are used in the classroom to help children control and channel their emotions positively. To help children settle down at class meetings, the teachers have the children do deep breathing while counting on their fingers. Or they invite the whole class to focus on a jar filled with glitter that is turned upside down until all of the glitter reaches the bottom. These approaches help children to settle "their inner tornadoes" and gain composure before the start of a meeting so that they can give the classwork their full attention.

Gratitude. Children are regularly encouraged to recognize and appreciate one another through such practices as a "round the circle" handshake at the end of the day that expresses their appreciation of one another. One child will shake another's hand, saying, "Thank you, Kofi, for being a part of our community." Kofi will return the handshake and comment by saying back, "Thank you, Marissa, for being a part of our community." Then Kofi will turn to the person on his other side and do the same, sometimes adding, "Thank you, Amari, for being my friend and for being part of our community." And the process goes on until everyone has had an opportunity to shake someone's hand and express gratitude. This ritual creates a sense of peace and acceptance among the group. It is then followed by a simple goodbye song, which is sung in multiple languages reflecting the diversity of cultures in the classroom.

PLAY, ACTIVE LEARNING, AND COMMUNITY BUILDING

Play and active learning have a prominent role in Vanessa and Kimberly's 1st/2nd-grade classroom.

Children Learn Through Play

As Vanessa explains:

> Play is important for many, many reasons. One is the opportunity to talk through things and be loud, which you don't often get at school. . . . Kids learn a lot from negotiating play—taking turns or even in their imaginative play, from little things like how many princesses there can be in the game to sharing blocks and things like that. There is that aspect also of just learning through work with materials. We see some pretty amazing engineering happen in this room as well as some art/creativity that surprises you in such young children. And . . . we try to give access to a nature table [Kimberly is great about bringing in lots of stuff from her hiking trips—kids get to play with things that they might not necessarily be able to touch living in the city].
>
> Kimberly continues:
>
> Play is essential in the 1st and 2nd grade because these grades are still a part of early childhood. In the educational system today, there is such a push to have kids reading at an earlier level and spending more time seated and working with paper and pencil that there is really a lot less time for kids to engage in play, whether it is individual or with their peers. And then there are the complications of technology, where more kids outside of the school day are spending their time connected and engaging in screen time, and they're missing out on those interactions and those social connections that they get through play. . . . Children learn from all of the interactions in play. Sometimes, if people observe it, they think, 'Oh, the kids are just playing and not learning,' but they are learning so much! They are experiencing new materials all the time. And they are having a lot of hands-on experience that they may not get someplace else. And the benefits from the conversations and navigating relationships with each other is essential. Trying to navigate conflicts

> and rules, and having conversations and play and role-playing and working out their own emotions through play—it is all essential to this age. And if we skip it now, it is going to come up later in their lives that they have missed this essential component.

To put into practice their belief about the importance of play to young children's learning, Kimberly and Vanessa's class offers some materials that are not generally found in 2nd grade. There are blocks, manipulative materials and games, a dollhouse, and a dramatic play area that has some baby dolls to take care of. Vanessa notes:

> What I have found very interesting in our class this year is that it is the boys who are going to the babies and the dollhouse the most. And I think that maybe they haven't had opportunities to play with those things before. It is a nice opportunity. There is such a push for boys to be engaged in rough-and-tumble play and to toughen up and to not show their emotions. But the dramatic play area offers them an opportunity to show their nurturing side.

Community Open Worktime

Vanessa and Kimberly's commitment to play for young children is put into practice every day when they provide a period called Open Worktime, a time when children can choose what they want to work on. To launch the worktime, the children first gather in the meeting area and sign up for what they want to do that day. Choices range from Legos, to reading, to dollhouse, to dramatic play, to blocks, to nature study, to writing, to math manipulatives.

Figure 16.1. Worktime Choices

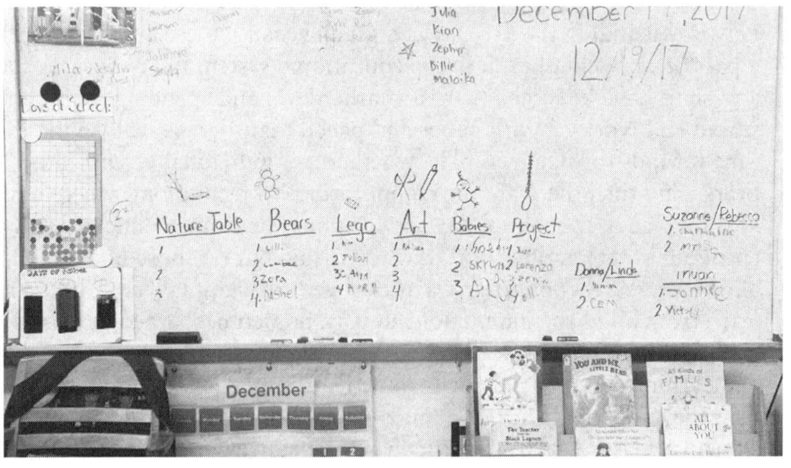

This choice time is extended to the entire school once a week when all of the grades have an Open Worktime at the same time. This is called Community Open Worktime (referred to as COW). During COW, children visit other classrooms and grades to work together or sometimes participate in clubs that happen at that time. During the year of this study, COW featured a 5th-grade student running an origami club. Each week, he went to each class to pick up a few children who wanted to participate. A dance club was offered, as well as a football club and a martial arts club. Sometimes the 2nd-graders will choose to visit the 3rd grade to check out what is in store for them in the future. Or sometimes the children will select to visit their past classrooms to be with old friends and their past teacher and to use remembered favorite materials.

COW is also a time that opens the door for family involvement. Any family member who has special skills or knowledge that they want to share with the school or the class in particular can come in and have a group to work with during COW. For example, one parent conducted a Spanish club, and another offered face painting.

Overall, Community Open Worktime serves as a community-building experience for the entire school.

Learning Skills in an Activity-Based Classroom

People often ask Kimberly and Vanessa how the important literacy, math, and other content-area skills and knowledge expected of children in 1st and 2nd grade are taught in their activity-based classroom.

Literacy Learning. One part of their reply, backed up by research (Ravachew, 2010; Shonkoff, 2017; Snow, 1983), is that early literacy skills develop through language exchanges, with talking and listening being an important foundation. In that regard, the talking and listening that children do while engaged in play is a big part of literacy learning. The teachers also explain that having rich and varied experiences in the world is also an important prerequisite of literacy. Readers need background knowledge to help them make sense of texts. That is how all the play, all the materials with which children engage, and all the trips and walks that they take contribute to a general knowledge base needed for the development of literacy skills.

But children do not learn skills in Vanessa and Kimberly's classroom only through play and hands-on activities. The class also regularly holds reading workshops in which literacy lessons in phonics and other skills are explicitly taught and a lot of stories are read (many of which focus on the social/emotional issues the teachers emphasize in their classroom). Small guided-reading groups are held every day so that the teachers can meet children where they are on the literacy development continuum and move forward from there rather than giving everyone the same assignment. Times devoted to writing workshop (Fletcher & Portalupi, 2001) are also a regular part of the class schedule.

Math Learning. Daily small-group math work is done as well. A developmental approach is applied to all of the lessons. Games are a big part of that work. For math, in particular, a lot of time is spent working with manipulatives and experiencing math through real-life problem solving. The rationale behind this approach is to ensure that the children are not just putting paper to pencil and solving equations in a rote manner, but that they are developing understandings of what they are doing.

Skill Learning Through the Exchange of Ideas. Children also learn skills in Vanessa and Kimberly's active classroom through the sharing of ideas that takes place in the community. They all learn that it is okay to use and build on someone else's ideas; in fact, impacting one another's ideas is what group learning is about. As Vanessa explains:

> We encourage the community to share ideas and listen to one another. We really have to work hard to create a community that can do that, where people feel safe in sharing an idea even though it might not be the 'correct' answer. We try to help the children understand that their idea might take us toward an answer or may give us other new ideas. Sharing an idea and then following it with conversations, letting the kids lead the conversations, debating if you have a different idea, asking why you think this idea should be valued more than this one, or questioning how you come up with your idea—this kind of sharing leads to bigger conversation.

The Billion Oyster Project. During the time of this study in Vanessa and Kimberly's classroom, an oyster study was begun, with plans to infuse it into the curriculum. Kimberly brought in the project as a result of her participation in the Billion Oysters project, a citywide initiative to put a billion oysters in the waterways of New York City. This initiative was modeled on the city's effort to plant a million trees in the city to not only beautify it but also to combat pollution. Putting oysters back into the New York waterways is an effort to filter the waterways—one oyster can filter 25 gallons of water per day—as well as to bring attention to the effects of human pollution on earth systems.

The oysters that Kimberly brought into the classroom were placed in a tank in the classroom where they will live. Kimberly also has oysters that are in a cage in the East River. She will lead the class on trips to the river in the spring to observe and document what happens to those river oysters. The purpose behind bringing oysters into the classroom is based on the foundational principles of their classroom and school: to care for one another and the earth. It also aligns with the curriculum of learning about the neighborhood, the community, and how people interact with each other in New York City. As Kimberly explains:

> Oysters were a big part of that early foundation of New York's existence. So, what does that mean? What happened to the oysters? How can we bring them back? Along with that work, the kids get a lot of hands-on experiences. They thrive with the excitement of getting to look at and touch things and investigate.

Figure 16.2. Oyster Chart

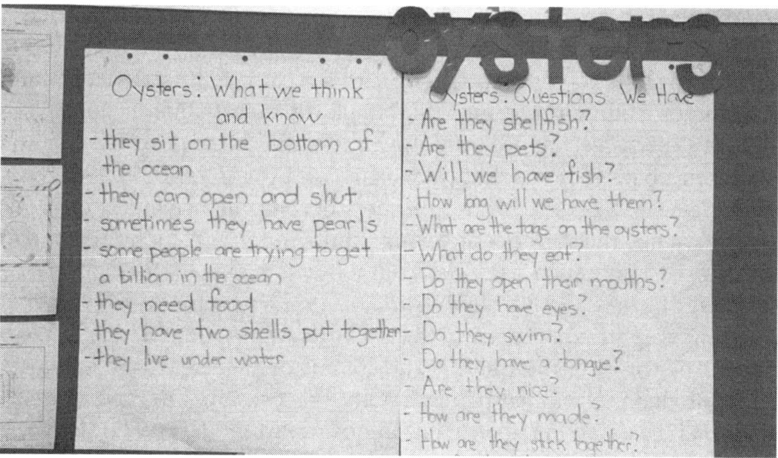

PRACTICING DEMOCRACY

The community-building strategies and initiatives that Kimberly and Vanessa use in their classroom contribute not only to a disciplined and caring environment but they also strengthen the learning that takes place. Through the combination of play and active learning and a focus on social and emotional responsiveness, children are supported to inquire and engage in the deep thinking needed to learn about and understand the world around them, to respect and care for one another, and to think about the implications of their actions for our collective human community. What better way to prepare our youngsters to sustain an equitable and just democracy than by practicing it daily in the classroom?

CHAPTER 17

Partnering with Families in School Life

Parents/families are a child's first teacher. All policies regarding families in a school need to be guided by this fact. We educators must not forget that families have important understandings about their children that need to be valued, that children come to school with a wealth of knowledge from their backgrounds and cultures, and that since learning builds on prior knowledge and experience, we need to know about and be respectful of all aspects of children's backgrounds that they bring with them to school.

The research is clear that children's development is maximized when they experience the support of caring adults in families, schools, and communities (Brown & Reeve, 1987; Gonzalez et al., 2005; Rogoff, 2003; Sampson, Sharkey, & Raudenbush, 2007). The social and economic environment in which children grow up (prenatally into the early years of life) affects not only the quality and extent of their learning but also the quality of their relationships, especially the primary caregiving relationship, which has a powerful impact on how children develop and what they learn (Bowman, Donovan, & Burns, 2001; Shonkoff & Phillips, 2000). Close and dependable early relationships that provide love, nurturance, and security; are responsive to needs; foster connections; and encourage engagement and exploration are what promote optimal development. When children do not have such a nurturing environment—or at least one close and dependable relationship—their development can be seriously disrupted (Garborino, Dubrow, Kostelny, & Pardo, 1998; Shonkoff & Phillips, 2000).

Putting this knowledge into effect in schools means involving families as partners in the learning community and engaging them in a variety of ways to play an important role in supporting their children's learning. Besides making the school accessible to families, opportunities also need to be provided to enhance families' understandings of the educational philosophy and practices of the school, especially when these practices differ from the ways that family members have been educated in the past. The more family members understand and support what goes on in school, the more they will be able to assist their children's learning (Epstein & Sanders, 2018; Falk, 2008).

This chapter offers suggestions for how to nurture home–school partnerships through a variety of communication mechanisms and structures.

COMMUNICATION VEHICLES BUILD COMMUNITY

Developing multiple avenues for communication between home and school helps to build common goals and understandings between families and teachers and thus a more effective and cohesive educational community. Communication avenues need to exist at both the classroom and the school level. At the classroom level, these can include teacher curriculum letters, questionnaires, phone calls to family members, homework notes, progress reports, family conferences, and class meetings. At the school level, communication can be facilitated through newsletters from the director or principal, through the parents' association, and by convening all-school meetings with families.

Teacher Curriculum Letters and Homework Notes

Communication from teachers to families about the learning that is taking place in the classroom is essential to strong home–school partnerships. A class "curriculum letter" (sent on a weekly, biweekly, or monthly basis), which contains written explanations of the studies and activities taking place in the classroom, can be a helpful way to share what is happening. Classroom newsletters can offer highlights of recent learning experiences, explain different educational practices (for example, what the "morning meeting" time of the day is and how it promotes literacy skills), and make suggestions to caregivers about how to support children's academic learning (for example, helpful hints for reading aloud to children, for how to choose appropriate books, for how to introduce a new book, for how to listen to children read, etc.). Below is an excerpt from a kindergarten teacher's curriculum letter that embodies some of these qualities.

Figure 17.1. Curriculum Letter

Dear Families of Kindergarten Students,

We will be working on the following units in Reading and Writing Workshop this month:

Reading Workshop Unit: Partner Talk & Comprehension
Writing Workshop Unit: Personal Narrative

Here are some ways to support the work your child is doing in these units at home:

(Continued)

Figure 17.1. Curriculum Letter *(continued)*

Reading Workshop:

- After reading a book with or to your child, have them talk to you about what happened in the story.
- Talk with your child about funny/sad/happy parts of the stories you read together.
- Have your child try to figure out words in the books using the first letter, last letter, and the picture.

Writing Workshop:

- Write stories about their lives.
- Practice writing a sentence.
- Practice spelling out new words by sounding out the letters.

Math Workshop:

- Look for 3D shapes at home.
- Talk about how 2D and 3D shapes are different.

It is important that we continue to work together for your child's success, and should you have any questions please do not hesitate to contact your child's teacher.

Sincerely,
Kindergarten Teachers

Sometimes teachers also use their curriculum letters to share resources they think might be of interest to families, such as helpful parenting tips or an inspirational poem. Or they ask parents to fill out questionnaires that provide information to enhance the teachers' knowledge of each child. Here is an example of such a questionnaire sent out to kindergarten families toward the beginning of the school year:

1. How does your child feel about coming to kindergarten? How do you feel? Do you have any special concerns?
2. Has your child been to other schools before? Where? For how long? How was the experience?
3. Are there other children in the family? How do they get along?
4. What kinds of things does your child like best to do? Active or quiet?
5. Does your child like books yet? Is she or he read to? How often? What are his or her favorites?
6. How is your child's appetite? Any food allergies? Food aversions? Are there school snacks we should avoid?
7. Any health problems?

Sometimes teachers send notes to ask families to participate in events or contribute needed items for the class. Here is a letter sent to solicit family involvement in classroom life:

> Dear Families,
>
> There are many opportunities for families to become involved in our classroom life. Let us know how you might like to participate. Please check all that apply and include any particulars:
>
> I can participate in class trips. Mon., Tues., Wed., etc.
> I can help with sewing.
> I would like to volunteer in the classroom to help with cooking or special projects.
> I know how to use a computer and can help with "publishing" children's work.
> I would like to share my job or talent with the class.

Teachers can communicate in other ways, too. Letters that accompany homework can explain the purpose and the skills embedded in it, and they can include instructions for how caregivers can help their children with assignments. Because teaching methods today are often different from those experienced by caregivers when they were in school, suggestions for how to support children with their homework can often make a critical difference in children's learning. These suggestions help, for example, to prevent children from getting confused because they receive one message from their families about how to do subtraction ("carry the one") when the school is teaching a different way (that the one in the tens column really represents a ten).

Figure 17.2. Homework Letter

READING HOMEWORK

Each and every afternoon or evening, your child's homework is to read for at least 15 minutes. No matter what other homework is assigned, this homework is to be done every day.

By reading, we mean that your child is either

- being read to;
- reading to you or another family member;
- reading on their own and/or browsing through and exploring books, magazines, newspapers, and other reading materials; or
- reading poems and songs given to them in class.

By rereading and learning this material your child will have many chances to experience success as a reader.

(Continued)

Figure 17.2. Homework Letter *(continued)*

HOMEWORK BOOKS

Your child will soon begin borrowing books from our classroom library for his or her daily reading homework. Your child will choose his or her own books. Many books we have read together in class and some may be new to your child. He or she may read a book more than once.

- If your child picks a book that they would like to read to you, and they are able, their homework is to read the book to you.
- If your child picks a book that they can read with some help, their homework is to read it along with you.
- If your child picks a book which they cannot read by themselves at all, their homework is to listen to you read it to them.

All books must be returned to school the next day. Returning books and selecting books will become part of your child's morning routine at school. Our goal is to have your child bring a book home to read every night. If for some reason your child has not returned his or her book she may not be allowed to take another book. In this way we will not lose track of books.

The children have been very anxious to bring books home to read. This is a big responsibility—borrowing a book to read for homework and returning it the very next day. Your child will need your help in developing the habit of caring for these books. The homework books will be sent home in heavy duty zip lock bags. Please teach your child to carefully put the book into the zip lock bag and then into his or her book bag as soon as he or she has finished reading. It is important that your child brings his or her book bag to school every day in order to protect the homework books borrowed. This will help to avoid damage and loss. There will be a $5 fee to replace lost books.

Whatever the communication method used to share information with families, it should be translated, whenever possible, into the languages represented in the class. And to enhance the flow of communication between home and school, a system can be set up to ensure that the curriculum letters, homework letters, and other important school messages are gathered in one place and actually get home. A "take-home folder" for each child is an effective way to do this. Caregivers can be asked to sign a return slip, usually attached to the letter, to indicate that the message has been read.

Class Meetings

Meetings between a classroom teacher and students' family members are a useful way for members of the classroom community to get acquainted with one another and to have an opportunity to address their questions and concerns. Most schools hold such gatherings in the form of "Open School Night" several times during the year. These meetings can be a vehicle for discussion about issues in the classroom, school, or education in general.

They can offer an opportunity for the class community to explore topics of interest such as literacy development, math, testing, conflict resolution, communication and discipline skills, sibling rivalry, health education, or issues related to cultural diversity. Whether led by the class teacher, outside "experts," or representatives of the school staff, meetings about educational issues can serve as forums for ongoing discussion of the classroom's teaching philosophy, values, and practices.

At such meetings, teachers can also invite family members to partake in the same activities that the children do during the day to give a feel for what the children's school experience is like. For example, caregivers can get a chance to build with blocks, work with math manipulatives, participate in a class meeting, and use other materials that the children engage with in class. Hands-on experiences like these for parents and guardians bring understandings about learning to life in deeper ways than just talking about them.

To ensure maximum attendance at family meetings, it is helpful to hold them in the evenings to accommodate parents and caregivers who work during the day. While this time may be good for those families who work, it presents other challenges such as child care and transportation. These challenges can be addressed in several ways: For those families for whom it is a hardship to pay for the additional round-trip transportation that an evening meeting would require, a transportation fund could be set up. Those in need could get reimbursed for their bus, subway, or car fare. Likewise, for families who have no one to stay with their children, child care could be provided at the meeting site. If children are present, the meetings could be held early so that everyone can get home at a reasonable hour. To make it easier for everyone to get to the school at an early hour, meetings could be preceded by a potluck supper. Attention to these issues can enhance participation.

Providing Resources from the School About Teaching and Learning

In addition to informing families about day-to-day happenings that are taking place in the school, it can be helpful to send home notes that explain to families the implications or underlying purposes of the educational practices in the classroom. These can help them gain new perspectives on such topics as literacy development, new standards for mathematics, and/or the problems of standardized tests. These notes can also include articles about an educational issue from a magazine, journal, or other educational resource, or suggestions for caregivers (lists of good multicultural books, for example). In addition, teachers can share ideas for how to handle issues pertaining to child development and parenting concerns, such as discipline, the stress children experience leading up to holiday time, concerns about excessive screen time, how to handle children's questions about sensitive subjects, or how to communicate with children in constructive ways.

These multiple forums for communication enable educators to share ideas and invite parents and guardians to express their questions and concerns, with the overall goal being to come to an understanding of one another's perspectives. Doing this is critical to developing the family support that is essential for teaching philosophies and practices to endure.

Other ways to stay connected to families are putting together a directory of all families in the classroom so that everyone can easily contact one another, bringing educational workshops to the class or school, making resources available (health, parenting, GED, language supports, immigration counseling, etc.), or seeking out resources for children—summer camps, after-school tutoring programs, and educational programs at the public library, local colleges, or community institutions. Notifying families of important community meetings, distributing literature about educational issues, and bringing resources (such as free-book programs) into the school also enrich everyone's lives.

Using Families' Resources and Funds of Knowledge in the Classroom

As noted in earlier chapters, utilizing the resources and knowledge of families also strengthens home–school partnerships. Families can be recruited to organize activities such as parties, breakfasts, concerts, and cultural performances. Events like these are opportunities for families to socialize together with their children in fun and educational contexts. Families can participate in and contribute to the classroom or school in other ways as well. Examples include a parent who is a nurse presenting a first-aid workshop; a parent who is a graphic designer creating a logo, t-shirt, and calendar for the class or school; a workshop on newspaper writing given to the children by a parent who is a journalist; a parent who is an amateur juggler giving a performance; and a parent who is a carpenter making frames for a paper-making project. Other family members can make other contributions: bringing a dancer friend to conduct a workshop with the class or bringing a relative to share dance or drumming representative of their country.

Parents and guardians can also participate by bringing their cultural resources to the curriculum: cooking a special family recipe or leading a special art project with the class, sharing music or telling stories from their culture (see Figure 2.16), donating needed supplies, and/or helping out in the classroom in other ways. Families can also publish their own communications to share information about interesting events in their community (school board elections or Family Day at El Museo del Barrio), news about community members' lives, information they have about useful services or resources, articles about parenting or education, or questionnaires developed by caregivers that ask for feedback on events, the curriculum, fund-raising activities, or suggestions for how people might want to get more involved. Feedback from families can be a crucial barometer to guide future activities and actions.

Parents and guardians can also help to raise funds for the classroom or school through such events as plant sales, book fairs, tree and wreath sales, holiday potlucks, or the annual sale of a calendar featuring the children's artwork. They can also organize activities that model for children how to help others, such as a household item drive for homeless people, food collection for those in need, support for those suffering from natural disasters, and so on.

MAXIMIZING AND SUSTAINING FAMILY INVOLVEMENT

Family involvement can be promoted, strengthened, and supported in the everyday life of the classroom. To do this, educators can use the following questions as a guide:

- What are the strengths of the families?
- What are the needs of families?
- How do we identify those strengths and needs?
- What encourages or discourages parents and caregivers to voice their concerns or to get involved?
- Given the diversity in a classroom, how do we ensure that families of all configurations from all racial, linguistic, economic, educational, and gender backgrounds are encouraged and welcomed to fully participate?

Challenges

Responses from families to the questions listed previously can provide teachers with rich information to use in mapping out comprehensive partnership plans. The challenge then is to find ways to build trusting relationships so that families actually *do* get involved. Because the involvement of families in most schools has traditionally been confined to arenas peripheral to educational matters, we need to ask ourselves how can barriers between families and school authorities be overcome? And how can opportunities for involvement be set up to accommodate the busy lives that most families experience?

Another challenge to consider is that when families *do* get a chance to have more access and input into the educational life of a classroom or school, confusion, uncertainty, and difficulties can arise because this is such unfamiliar territory. Parameters of power may not be clear, and as a result, boundaries and roles can get blurred. Finding the right balance between families' and educators' perspectives on educational philosophy, teaching methods, and curriculum development is not always easy.

The multiple forums for communication that have been described in this chapter can help to hash out differences, develop new insights, solidify connections, and strengthen relationships. While the road may be bumpy at times, it is incumbent on educators to explain our views thoroughly to the families in our communities so that plans and actions are well understood, connect to shared values, and make sense to all. Only by doing this will educators' actions have any chance of garnering the community's support.

Learning from Teaching

As has been described in these chapters, high-quality early learning is the result of teaching the way children learn. This kind of teaching

- creates meaningful and purposeful contexts for learning (within which is embedded explicit attention to the important content and skills children will need to contribute to our changing world);
- engages children in active experiences that build on their interests and utilize their strengths for the purpose of developing their deep understandings;
- integrates the curriculum to enable children to make connections between and among ideas;
- expects and supports everyone to develop the ability to think critically, to investigate and evaluate ideas, to be respectful of the perspectives of others, and to communicate and defend their thoughts orally and in writing;
- is respectful of and responsive to diversity;
- assesses children's learning through multiple measures that inform instruction and support children's learning;
- builds a community of care that pays attention to all aspects (social, emotional, physical, and cognitive) of the whole child; and
- involves families meaningfully in the life of the school.

There is no one right way to engage in this kind of teaching. Those who want to do it must discover their own path toward it, using their intelligence and creativity to shape what they do in response to the particularities of their context. However, an important part of the journey toward this goal is learning from the teaching experience itself. And that too is an element of providing a high-quality early learning environment: educators who, as they place children's needs at the center of classroom life, build professional community, nurture professional collaborations, and are engaged in continual learning.

THE TEACHING LIFE IS A LEARNING LIFE

Most people think of learning as a process that is done through books or in classes or from teachers and peers. But many overlook the powerful experience that learning through teaching can provide. This kind of learning can take place in several ways.

One way to ensure that you really understand a concept is to try to teach it to someone else. Teaching forces you to communicate your thoughts clearly and precisely. Your ideas will never be more effective than your ability to make others comprehend them. Teaching helps you develop the important skill of conveying your ideas well enough for others to use them.

Another way of learning through teaching is by examining and analyzing the details involved in teaching (Falk & Blumenreich, 2005, 2012). Sometimes it is by looking closely at individual learners that we find understandings that can be applied to all learners. For example, careful observation can reveal that Daria loves to sing to herself while she works, or Tania gets disruptive when she's hungry, or Christopher works hard but can tire easily. These insights prompt us to adjust what we do to support the differing needs of our students. Additionally, careful observation can help us find out what learners really think. This can help us to better understand them and aid us in finding ways to help them learn. Rather than blaming children (for "not learning"), we need to take responsibility for finding out how they think, what they know, and what they have learned. In doing so we may find that some children have not had the prior experiences needed to understand a concept. Then we need to use these understandings to further their learning. We need to remember that children have a natural drive to learn. Careful listening, careful observation, and eliminating preconceived notions or prejudices so that we can see what is really going on are skills that can help us to help children progress in their learning.

Reflective and systematic inquiry into our own teaching—our problems, our mistakes, or our lack of knowledge—can also be rich opportunities for learning. For example, when exploring a particular topic or skill with children, we may realize we need to learn more about it. Or, when cleanup time goes awry, we may realize we need to be more directive and less laid-back. Or, when dealing with a child who is whiny, self-analysis may lead us to understand that we need to learn to be more patient. We learn from what works but also from what doesn't.

And then there are things we learn from our students about issues of the world that we may not have previously known: what it is like to be an immigrant, what it feels like to be homeless, the benefits and challenges of speaking a language other than English. Spending time with children throughout a school day and year gives us the opportunity—and the privilege—of getting a glimpse into lives and worlds that are new and different from our own. If we approach our teaching with an openness to learn, we can gain new understandings that can help us to shed prior assumptions, clichés, and stereotypes. We can learn to appreciate the uniqueness and value of each individual, learn to respect others' strengths and challenges, and move toward a greater connection with our human community.

LEARNING WITH OTHERS IN COMMUNITY

To sustain the learning that is possible from teaching, professional conversations, support, and community are key. Collectively, we need to find the right fit in the right school to support us to engage in professional learning: to learn how to better observe children; to learn how to look and what to look for; to collect, review, and reflect on data; to coordinate our curricula with our colleagues; to dialogue, collaborate, and problem-solve with others (Lieberman & Falk, 2007).

We all have a need for dialogue and collaboration—a need to talk over with each other in the course of our work what we see and what we think. We need to ask questions, pose problems, discuss dilemmas, question assumptions, interrogate knowledge, and explore issues that we find to be problematic. We all need this kind of help from each other to refine and deepen our practice. In order to do it, we need the same kinds of opportunities for reflection and support that we aim to give to children: ongoing processes of actively making knowledge about teaching and learning.

There are many ways to do this, both personally and collectively. Personally, we can seek support—from a colleague, a friend, or a mentor. Reading together, problem solving together, visiting each other's classrooms, and visiting classrooms outside of the school can contribute to ongoing growth. All-school meetings, grade-level meetings, cross-grade meetings, one-on-one coaching, study groups, fish-bowl experiences (where a group of teachers watches another teacher teach), descriptive reviews of a child or a piece of work, classroom team meetings, staff retreats, professional conferences, and workshops all can be places where this work can occur.

Through the process of dialogue and reflection, our outlook and philosophy of teaching continually evolve. As teachers, we always need to be learning. We should always be trying to outgrow ourselves, because teachers are never finished—we are always in the making.

The teacher who stays and sustains herself in the challenges of the work is thus a reflective practitioner who understands that teaching is a cycle of inquiry, that change takes time, and that the teaching life is ultimately a learning life.

PROBLEMS AS OPPORTUNITIES

When teachers provide opportunities in schools for children to investigate, inquire, and reflect, children are supported to discover their own curiosity and creativity. Through this process they not only gain knowledge and skills, but they also get excited about setting their own purposes for their work, they find pleasure in pursuing their own interests, and they delight in taking charge of their own learning.

In an analogous way, when we teachers engage in this same process, our imaginations are ignited to tackle the ever-changing problems and challenges that continually arise in schools. In the sometimes confusing midst of these challenges, it is important to remember that problems are intrinsic to the process—they are an inevitable part of teaching and learning. While it is easy to see a problem as a failure, especially to the person who is in the middle of struggling with it, the key to moving forward is to embrace it and use it as an opportunity to learn. Just as water flows around and over obstacles in its path, moving forward requires finding a way over and around the encountered difficulties. In this way, step by step, progress can inevitably be found.

This journey is not an easy one. But for all of you who have the courage and fortitude to take on and stay at this arduous task, rewards will come. They will come in the promise of the children and families whose lives you will touch. Through teaching, you have the opportunity to nourish children's capacities to think, to dream, to enact, and to realize possibilities for our collective future. You may not get to witness all of the results, but the power of the support that you give to children will surely stay in their hearts and minds. In this way, teaching is truly an act of hope.

It is to that hope that I dedicate this book: that the young learners we teachers and caregivers nurture each day will use their newfound skills and knowledge to help move our human community forward and contribute to a more just and equitable world.

> This is what we are about:
> We plant seeds that one day will grow.
> We water seeds already planted, knowing that they hold future promise.
> We lay foundations that will need further development.
> We provide yeast that produces effects beyond our capabilities.
> We cannot do everything; and there is a sense of liberation in realizing that.
> This enables us to do something, and to do it very well.
> It may be incomplete, but it is a beginning, a step along the way . . .
> We may never see the end results; but this is the difference between the master builder and the worker.
> We are workers, not master builders; ministers, not messiahs.
> We are prophets of a future not our own.
>
> —From a homily written by Bishop Ken Untener (1979)

Methodology for Teaching Descriptions

The descriptions of teaching in Chapters 6, 8, 9, 11, and 16 came from a study of high-quality early learning that took place between 2015 and 2018, supported by the Foundation for Child Development. The teachers were selected to participate in the study based on the fact that they teach in culturally, racially, and socioeconomically diverse public schools that have significant percentages of students who are emergent bilinguals, who have special needs, and who are from low-income backgrounds (as per information on insideschools.org). The teachers were recommended by teacher educators and other educational leaders as demonstrating developmentally appropriate/culturally responsive practices (Copple & Bredekamp, 2009; Ladson-Billings, 2006).

A grounded theory approach (Glaser & Strauss, 1967) was used to analyze the data collected. Inductive and deductive axial coding of fieldnotes, interview transcriptions, videos, and documents identified themes supported by relevant excerpts of data; related categories to their subcategories; and interrogated data for disconfirming evidence. A member check with the participant-observer finalized the analysis. Data sources included the following:

- Fieldnotes and video of classroom observations of a unit of study documented over the course of several months. The classroom was visited 8 times for 3–4 hours each (6 mornings, 2 afternoons).
- Brief informal interviews with the teacher were conducted at each visit to provide context for the observations and to address clarifying questions.
- A semi-structured 45-minute interview with the teacher at the study's conclusion. This provided evidence about her perspectives and the organizational structures and policies impacting her teaching.
- Teacher's curriculum plans, notes, assessments, and letters to families to provide insights into her planning and thinking.
- Samples of children's work from the study to demonstrate the quality of the learning.

References

Adams, M. J. (1998). The three-cueing system. In F. Lehr & J. Osborn (Eds.), *Literacy for all issues in teaching and learning* (pp. 73–99). New York, NY: Guilford Press.

Adams, M. J., Foorman, B. R., Lundberg, I., & Beeler, T. (1998). The elusive phoneme: Why phonemic awareness is so important and how to help children develop it. *American Educator, 22*(1–2), 18–29.

Akers, E. (2014). *Five ways to keep it developmentally appropriate—Part I.* Retrieved from www.gesellinstitute.org/8-5-14-five-ways-keep-developmentally-appropriate-part-i/

American Academy of Pediatrics. (2013). The crucial role of recess in school. *Pediatrics, 131*(1). Retrieved from http://pediatrics.aappublications.org/content/131/1/183

Atwell, N. (1989). *Coming to know: Writing to learn in the intermediate grades.* Portsmouth, NH: Heinemann.

Au, K., & Jordan, C. (1981). Teaching reading to Hawaiian children: Finding a culturally appropriate solution. In H. Tureba, G. Guthrie, & K. Au (Eds.), *Culture and the bilingual classroom: Studies in classroom ethnography* (pp. 139–152). Rowley, MA: Newbury House.

Ballenger, C. (1998). *Teaching other people's children: Literacy and learning in a bilingual classroom.* New York, NY: Teachers College Press.

Banks, J. (2006). *Race, culture, and education: The selected works of James A. Banks.* London & New York, NY: Routledge.

Barnett, W. S. (1995). Long-term effects of early childhood programs on cognitive and school outcomes. *Future of Children, 5*(3), 25–50.

Bassok, D., Latham, S., & Rorem, A. (2016, January 6). Is kindergarten the new first grade? *AERA Open.* Retrieved from www.aera.net/Newsroom/News-Releases-and-Statements/Study-Snapshot-Is-Kindergarten-the-New-First-Grade/Is-Kindergarten-the-New-First-Grade

Berger, K. (2008). *The developing person through childhood and adolescence* (8th ed.). New York, NY: Worth Publishers.

Bodrova, E., & Leong, D. J. (2007). *Tools of the mind: The Vygotskian approach to early childhood education* (2nd ed.). New York, NY: Pearson.

Bowman, B. T., Donovan, M. S., & Burns, M. S. (Eds.). (2001). *Eager to learn: Educating our preschoolers.* Washington, DC: National Academy Press.

Bransford, J. D., Brown, A. L., & Cocking, R. R. (Eds.). (2000). *How people learn: Brain, mind, experience, and school.* Washington, DC: National Academy of Sciences.

Brophy, J. E. (2013). *Motivating students to learn.* New York, NY: Routledge.

Brown, A. L., & Campione, J. C. (1996). Psychological theory and the design of innovative learning environments: On procedures, principles, and systems. In L. Schauble & R. Glaser (Eds.), *Innovations in learning: New environments for education* (pp. 289–325). Mahwah, NJ: Erlbaum.

Brown, A. L., & Reeve, R. A. (1987). Bandwiths of competence: The role of supportive contexts in learning and development. In L. S. Liben (Ed.), *The Jean Piaget Symposium series. Development and learning: Conflict or congruence?* (pp. 173–223). Hillsdale, NJ: Lawrence Erlbaum Associates.

Brown, S. L. (2009). *Play: How it shapes the brain, opens the imagination, and invigorates the soul.* New York, NY: Avery, Penguin Group.

Bruner, J. (1995). From joint attention to the meeting of minds: An introduction. In C. Moore, P. Dunham, & J. Bruner (Eds.), *Joint attention: Its origins and role in development.* New York, London: Psychology Press.

Byers-Heinlein, K., & Lew-Williams, C. (2013). Bilingualism in the early years: What the science says. *LEARNing Landscapes, 7*(1), 95–112.

Calkins, L. M. (1994). *The art of teaching writing.* New York, NY: Pearson.

Calkins, L. M. (2000). *The art of teaching reading.* New York, NY: Pearson.

Cambourne, C. (2002). The conditions of learning: Is learning natural? *The Reading Teacher 55*(8), 758–762.

Cazden, C. B., & John, V. P. (1971). Learning in American Indian children. In M. L. Wax, S. Diamond, & F. O. Hearing (Eds.), *Anthropological perspectives on education* (pp. 252–272). New York, NY: Basic Books.

Center on the Developing Child. (2017). *Brain architecture.* Retrieved from developingchild.harvard.edu/science/key-concepts/brain-architecture/

Clements, D. H., & Sarama, J. (2011). Early childhood mathematics intervention. *Science, 333*(6045), 968–970.

Cohen, D., Stern, V., Balaban, N., & Gropper, N. (2015). *Observing and recording the behavior of young children.* New York, NY: Teachers College Press.

Common Core State Standards. (2015). *Common core state standards.* Retrieved from www.corestandards.org

Copple, C., & Bredekamp, S. (Eds.). (2009). *Developmentally appropriate practice in early childhood programs serving children from birth through age 8.* (3rd ed.) Washington, DC: NAEYC.

Cordova, D. I., & Lepper, M. R. (1996). Intrinsic motivation and the process of learning: Beneficial effects of contextualization, personalization, and choice. *Journal of Educational Psychology, 88*(4), 715.

Costa, A. L., & Kallick, B. (2009). *Habits of mind across the curriculum: Practical and creative strategies for teachers.* Washington, DC: Association for Curriculum Development.

Cummins, J. (2001). *Language, power, and pedagogy: Bilingual children in the crossfire*. Clevedon, UK: Multilingual Matters Limited.

Damasio, A. R. (1994). *Descartes' error: Emotion, reason, and the human brain*. New York, NY: G. P. Putnam.

Danese, A., Moffitt, T., Harrington, H., Milne, B., Polanczyk, G., Pariante, C., . . . Caspi, A. (2009). Adverse childhood experiences and adult risk factors for age-related disease. *Archives of Pediatrics and Adolescent Medicine, 163*, 1135–1143.

Darling-Hammond, L. (1997). *The right to learn: A blueprint for school reform*. San Francisco, CA: Jossey-Bass.

Darling-Hammond, L. (2008). *Powerful learning: What we know about teaching for understanding*. San Francisco, CA: Jossey-Bass.

Darling-Hammond, L. (2010). *The flat world and education: How America's commitment to equity will determine our future*. New York, NY: Teachers College Press.

Darling-Hammond, L. (2015). *Teaching in the flat world: Learning from high performing systems*. New York, NY: Teachers College Press.

Darling-Hammond, L., Ancess, J., & Falk, B. (1995). *Authentic assessment in action*. New York, NY: Teachers College Press.

Delpit, L. (1988). The silenced dialogue: Power and pedagogy in educating other people's children. *Harvard Educational Review, 58*(3), 280–299.

Dewey, J. (1914). Reasoning in early childhood. In P. S. Hill (Ed.), *Experimental studies in kindergarten theory and practice* (p. 1). Reprinted in *Teachers College Record 15*(1). New York, NY: Teachers College, Columbia University.

Dewey, J. (1916). *Democracy and education*. New York, NY: Macmillan.

Dewey, J. (1938). *Education and experience*. New York, NY: Macmillan.

Diamond, A., Barnett, W. S., Thomas, J., & Munro, S. (2007). Preschool program improves cognitive control. *Science, 318*, 1387–1388.

Dickinson, D. K., & Tabors, P. O. (2001). *Beginning literacy with language*. Baltimore, MD: Brookes Publishing.

Early Math Collaborative, Erikson Institute. (2014). *Big ideas of early mathematics: What teachers of young children need to know*. Hackensack, NJ: Pearson.

Edwards, C., Gandini, L., & Forman, G. (Eds.). (1998). *Hundred languages of children: The Reggio Emilia approach to early childhood education* (2nd ed.). Westport, CT: Ablex Publishing.

Elango, S., García, J. L., Heckman, J. J., & Hojman, A. (2015). *Early childhood education* (No. w21766). National Bureau of Economic Research.

Elbow, P., & Belanoff, P. (1986). Portfolios as a substitute for proficiency examinations. *College Composition and Communication, 37*(3), pp. 336–339.

Elkind, D. (2001). *The hurried child: Growing up too fast too soon* (3rd ed.). New York, NY: Persius Publishing

Elstgeest, J. (1985). The right question at the right time. In W. Harlen (Ed.), *Primary science: Taking the plunge* (pp. 36–46). Oxford, England: Heinemann Educational.

Epstein, J., & Sanders, M. G. (2018). *School, family, and community partnerships: Your handbook for action* (4th ed.). Thousand Oaks, CA: Corwin Press.

Erikson, E. (1963). *Childhood and society*. New York, NY: Norton.

Falk, B. (2000). *The heart of the matter: Using standards and assessments to learn*. Portsmouth, NH: Heinemann Press.

Falk, B. (2008). *Teaching the way children learn*. New York, NY: Teachers College Press.

Falk, B. (2012). *Defending childhood: Keeping the promise of early childhood education*. New York, NY: Teachers College Press.

Falk, B., & Blumenreich, M. (2005). *The power of questions: A guide to teacher and student research*. Portsmouth, NH: Heinemann Press.

Falk, B., & Blumenreich, M. (2012). *Teaching matters: Stories from inside city schools*. New York, NY: The New Press.

Falk, B., Gropper, N., & Shore, R. (2017). *Joining with the learner: A strategy for strengthening early childhood education*. New York, NY: New York City Early Childhood Exchange.

Fletcher, R., & Portalupi, J. (2001). *Writing workshop: The essential guide*. Portsmouth, NH: Heinemann.

Fountas, I., & Pinnell, G. S. (2001). *Guiding readers and writers/grades 3–6*, Portsmouth, NH: Heinemann.

Fountas, I., & Pinnell, G. S. (2016). *The Fountas & Pinnell literacy continuum, expanded edition: A tool for assessment, planning, and teaching, preK–8*. Portsmouth, NH: Heinemann Press.

Freire, P. (2005). *Teachers as cultural workers: Letters to those who dare teach*. Boulder, CO: Westview Press.

Froebel, F. (1826/2005). *The education of man*. Mineola, NY: Dover Publications.

Fuller, B., Bein, E., Bridges, M., Kim, Y., & Rabe-Hesketh, S. (2017). Do academic preschools yield stronger benefits? Cognitive emphasis, dosage, and early learning. *Journal of Applied Developmental Psychology, 52*(in progress), 1–11.

Gao, H. (2005, April 11). Kindergarten or "kindergrind"? School getting tougher for kids. *San Diego Union Tribune*.

Garborino, J., Dubrow, N., Kostelny, K., & Pardo, C. (1998). *Children in danger: Coping with the consequences of community violence*. San Francisco, CA: Jossey-Bass.

García, E. E., & Frede, E. C. (2010). *Young English language learners: Current research and emerging directions for practice and policy*. New York, NY: Teachers College Press.

García, J. L., Heckman, J. J., Leaf, D. E., & Prados, M. J. (2017). *Quantifying the life-cycle benefits of a prototypical early childhood program* (No. w23479). National Bureau of Economic Research.

García, O., & Wei, L. (2014). *Translanguaging: Language, bilingualism and education*. New York, NY: Palgrave.

García, O., Johnson, S., & Seltzer, K. (2017). *The translanguaging classroom: Leveraging student bilingualism for learning*. Philadelphia: Caslon.

García, O., Lin, A. M. Y., & May, S. (2017). *Bilingual and multilingual education.* New York, NY: Springer International Publishing.

Gardner, H. (1983/2011). *Frames of mind: The theory of multiple intelligences.* New York, NY: Basic Books.

Gay, G. (2002). Preparing for culturally responsive teaching. *Journal of Teacher Education, 53*(20), 106–116.

Gay, G. (2010). *Culturally responsive teaching: Theory, research, and practice* (2nd ed.). New York, NY: Teachers College Press.

Gay, G. (2013). Teaching to and through cultural diversity. *Curriculum Inquiry, 43*(1), 48–70.

Genishi, C., & Dyson, A. H. (2009). *Children, language, and literacy: Diverse learners in diverse times.* New York, NY: Teachers College Press.

Gentry, R. (1987). *Spel . . . is a four-letter word.* Portsmouth, NH: Heinemann.

Gesell, A. (1925). *The mental growth of the pre-school child: A psychological outline of normal development from birth to the sixth year, including a system of developmental diagnosis.* New York, NY: Macmillan.

Gilliam, W., & Shahar, G. (2006). Prekindergarten expulsion and suspension: Rates and predictors in one state. *Infants and Young Children, 19*, 228–245.

Ginsberg, K. (2007). The importance of play in promoting healthy child development and maintaining strong parent-child bonds. *Pediatrics 119*(1), 182–191.

Glaser, B., & Strauss, A. (1967). *The discovery of grounded theory: Strategies for qualitative research.* New York, NY: Aldine.

Gonzalez, N., Moll, L. C., & Amanti, C. (Eds.). (2005). *Funds of knowledge: Theorizing practices in households and classrooms.* Mahwah, NJ: Lawrence Erlbaum Associates.

Greene, M. (1978). *Landscapes of learning.* New York, NY: Teachers College Press.

Grindal, T. A., Hinton, C., & Shonkoff, J. P. (2012). The science of early childhood development: Lessons for teachers and caregivers. In B. Falk (Ed.), *Defending childhood: Keeping the promise of early education* (pp. 13–23). New York, NY: Teachers College Press.

Guddemi, M. (2013, August 21). Important new findings linking self-regulation, pretend play and learning in young children. *SEEN Magazine.* Retrieved from seenmagazine.us/articles/article-detail/articleid/3237/important-new-findings .aspx.

Gunnar, M., Morison, S., Chisholm, K., & Schuder, M. (2001). Salivary cortisol levels in children adopted from Romanian orphanages. *Development and Psychopathology 13*(3), 611–628.

Hakuta, K., & Garcia, E. E. (1989). Bilingualism and education. *American Psychologist, 44*(2), 374–79.

Hanh, T. N. (1992). *Peace is every step: The path of mindfulness in everyday life.* New York, NY: Bantam. Retrieved from www.goodreads.com/quotes/153586 -when-you-plant-lettuce-if-it-does-not-grow-well

Harlen, W. (Ed.). (1985). *Primary science: Taking the plunge.* Portsmouth, NH: Heinemann.

Harlen, W., Darwin, A., & Murphy, M. (1977). *Match and mismatch: Fitting learning experiences in science to development for five to thirteen years old.* London, England: Oliver and Boyd for the Schools Council.

Harris, D. E., & Carr, J. F. (1996). *How to use standards in the classroom.* Alexandria, VA: Association for Supervision and Curriculum Development.

Hart, B., & Risley, T. R. (1995). *Meaningful differences in the everyday experience of young American children.* Baltimore, MD: Brookes Publishing.

Hawkins, D. (1965). Messing about in science. *Science and Children (2)5.* Retrieved from www.colorado.edu/ftep/sites/default/files/attached-files/ftep_memo_to_faculty_42.pdf

Heckman, J. J. (2012). The case for investing in young children. In B. Falk (Ed.), *Defending childhood: Keeping the promise of early education* (pp. 235–242). New York, NY: Teachers College Press.

Heckman, J., Pinto, R., & Savelyev, P. (2013). Understanding the mechanisms through which an influential early childhood program boosted adult outcomes. *American Economic Review, 103*(6), 2052–2086.

Hinton, C., Miyamoto, K., & della-Chiesa, B. (2008). Brain research, learning and emotions: Implications for education research, policy and practice. *European Journal of Education, 43*(1), 87–103.

Hirsch, E. (1974). *Transitions: A stumbling block to education.* Washington, DC: National Association for the Education of Young Children.

Hirsh-Pasek, K., Golinkoff, R. M., Berk, L. E., & Singer, D. G. (2009). *A mandate for playful learning: Presenting the evidence.* New York, NY: Oxford University Press.

Hymes, D. (1967). Models of the interaction of language and social setting. *Journal of Social Issues 23*(2), 8–28.

Irvine, J. (2003). *Education teachers for diversity: Seeing with a cultural eye.* New York, NY: Teachers College Press.

Jones, R. M. (1968). *Fantasy and feeling in education.* New York, NY: NYU Press.

Kaczmarek, L. (1997). *The neuron.* New York, NY: Oxford University Press.

Kagan, S. L., & Lowenstein, A. E. (2004). School readiness and children's play: Contemporary oxymoron or compatible option? In *Children's play: The roots of reading* (pp. 59–76). Washington, DC: Zero to Three.

Kagan, S. L., Scott-Little, C., & Frelow, F. (2009). Linking play to early learning and development guidelines: Possibility or polemic? *Zero to Three, 30*(1), 18–25.

Kamii, C. (1985). *Young children reinvent arithmetic.* New York, NY: Teachers College Press.

Kohn, A. (2004). *What does it mean to be well educated?* Boston, MA: Beacon Press.

Koplow, L. (2002). *Bears, bears, everywhere: Supporting children's emotional health in the classroom.* New York, NY: Teachers College Press.

Ladson-Billings, G. (1994). *The dreamkeepers: Successful teachers of African-American children.* San Francisco, CA: Jossey-Bass.

Ladson-Billings, G. (1995). Toward a theory of culturally relevant pedagogy. *American Educational Research Journal, 32*(3), 465–491.

Ladson-Billings, G. (2005). *Culturally-relevant teaching*. Mahwah, NJ: Lawrence Erlbaum.

Ladson-Billings, G. (2006). From the achievement gap to the education debt: Understanding achievement in U.S. schools. *Educational Researcher 35*(7), 3–12.

Lally, J. R., & Mangione, P. (2017). Caring relationships: The heart of early brain development. *Young Children 72*(2), 17–24.

Leong, D. J., & Bodrova, E. (2012). Assessing and scaffolding: Make-believe play. *Young Children 67*(1), 28–34.

Lieberman, A., & Falk, B. (2007). Leadership in learner-centered schools. In A. Danzig, K. Borman, B. Jones, & W. Wright (Eds.), *Professional development for learner centered leadership: Policy, research, and practice*. Mahway, NJ: Lawrence Erlbaum Associates.

Meisels, S. (2006). *Accountability in early childhood education: No easy answers*. Occasional Paper, 6. Chicago, IL: Herr Research Center, Erikson Institute.

Miller, E., & Almon, J. (2009). *Crisis in the kindergarten: Why children need to play in school*. College Park, MD: Alliance for Childhood.

Moffitt, T. E., Arseneault, L., Belsky, D., Dickson, N., Hancox, R. J., Harrington, . . . Caspi, A. (2011). A gradient of childhood self-control predicts health, wealth, and public safety. *Proceedings of the National Academy of Sciences, USA 108*(7), 2693–2698.

Moll, L. C., Amanti, C., Neff, D., & Gonzalez, N. (1992). Funds of knowledge for teaching: A qualitative approach to connect homes and schools. *Theory Into Practice 31*(2), 132–141.

National Association for the Education of Young Children. (1987). *Standardized testing of young children 3 through 8 years of age*. Washington, DC: NAEYC.

National Association for the Education of Young Children. (1998). *Learning to read and write: Developmentally appropriate practices for young children*. A joint position statement of the International Reading Association and the National Association for the Education of Young Children. Washington, DC: NAEYC.

National Association for the Education of Young Children (NAEYC). (2009). *Developmentally appropriate practice in early childhood programs serving children from birth through age 8*. Washington, DC: Author.

National Association for the Education of Young Children & National Association for Early Childhood Specialists in State Departments of Education. (2003). *Early childhood curriculum, assessment, and program evaluation* [Online joint position statement]. Retrieved from www.naeyc.org/about/positions/pdf/pscape.pdf

National Association of School Psychologists. (2005). *NASP position statement on early childhood assessment* [Online document]. Bethesda, MD: NASP. Retrieved from www.nasponline.org/information/pospaper_eca.html

National Council of Teachers of Mathematics. (2013). *Mathematics in early childhood learning*. Retrieved from www.nctm.org/Standards-and-Positions/Position-Statements/Mathematics-in-Early-Childhood-Learning/

National Research Council. (1998). *Preventing reading difficulties in young children.* Washington, DC: The National Academies Press. Retrieved from doi .org/10.17226/6023.

National Scientific Council on the Developing Child. (2004). *Young children develop in an environment of relationships* (Working Paper No. 1). Retrieved from www.developingchild.net

National Scientific Council on the Developing Child. (2005). *Excessive stress disrupts the architecture of the developing brain* (Working Paper No. 3). Retrieved from www.developingchild.harvard.edu

National Scientific Council on the Developing Child. (2007). *The science of early childhood development: Closing the gap between what we know and what we do.* Retrieved from www.developingchild.net/

National Scientific Council on the Developing Child. (2009). *Maternal depression can undermine the development of young children* (Working Paper No. 8). Retrieved from www.developingchild.harvard.edu

National Scientific Council on the Developing Child. (2010). *Persistent fear and anxiety can affect young children's learning and development* (Working Paper No. 9). Retrieved from www.developingchild.harvard.edu

Nelson, C. A., & Sheridan, M. A. (2011). Lessons from neuroscience research for understanding causal links between family and neighborhood characteristics and educational outcomes. In G. Duncan & R. Murnane (Eds.), *Whither opportunity?: Rising inequality, schools, and children's life chances* (pp. 27–46). New York, NY: Russell Sage Foundation Press.

New York State Education Department. (1999). *The early literacy profile.* Albany, NY: Author.

Next Generation Science Standards. (2016). *Next generation science standards.* Retrieved from www.nextgenscience.org/

Nichols, S. L., Glass, G. V., & Berliner, D. (2006). High-stakes testing and student achievement: Does accountability pressure increase student learning? *Education Policy Analysis Archives.* Retrieved from dx.doi.org/10.14507/epaa .v14n1.2006

Nieto, S., & Bode, P. (2012). *Affirming diversity: The sociopolitical context of multicultural education* (6th ed.). Boston, MA: Allyn & Bacon.

Noddings, N. (1984). *Caring: A feminine approach to ethics and moral education.* Berkeley: University of California Press.

Noddings, N. (2013). *Education and democracy in the 21st century.* New York, NY: Teachers College Press.

Nolte, D. L. (1972). *Children learn what they live.* Retrieved from www .empowermentresources.com/info2/childrenlearn-long_version.html

Pakulak, E., Gomsrud, M., Bell, T. A., Giuliano, R. J., Karns, C. M., Klein, S., . . . Neville, H. (2017). Focusing on families: A two-generation model for reducing parents' stress and boosting preschoolers' self-regulation and attention. *Young Children* 72(2), 25–37.

Palmer, P. J. (1998/2017). *The courage to teach: Exploring the inner landscape of a teacher's life* (20th anniversary ed.). San Francisco, CA: Jossey-Bass.

Paris, D., & Alim, H. S. (2017). *Culturally sustaining pedagogies: Teaching and learning for justice in a changing world.* New York, NY: Teachers College Press.

Perrone, V. (1991). *A letter to teachers.* San Francisco, CA: Jossey-Bass.

Philips, S. U. (2009). Participant structures and communicative competence: Warm Springs children in community and classroom. In A. Duranti (Ed.), *Linguistic anthropology: A reader* (2nd ed., pp. 329–342). Hoboken, NJ: Wiley.

Piaget, J. (1952). *The origins of intelligence in children.* New York, NY: International Universities Press.

Piaget, J. (1970). *Genetic epistemology.* New York, NY: Columbia University Press.

Piaget, J., & Inhedler, B. (1969). *The psychology of the child.* New York, NY: Basic Books.

Pianta, R., & Walsh, D. (2014). *High-risk children in schools: Constructing sustaining relationships.* New York, NY: Routledge.

Polakow, V. (2012). Foreclosed childhoods: Poverty, inequality, and discarding the young. In B. Falk (Ed.), *Defending childhood: Keeping the promise of early education* (pp. 89–113). New York, NY: Teachers College Press.

Pollak, S. D., Cicchetti, D., Hornung, K., & Reed, A. (2000). Recognizing emotion in faces: Developmental effects of child abuse and neglect. *Developmental Psychology, 36,* 679–688.

Purcell-Gates, V. (2007). *Cultural practices of literacy: Case studies of language, literacy, social practice, and power.* Mahwah, NJ: Lawrence Erlbaum Associates.

Ramirez, N. F., & Kuhl, P. (2017). The brain science of bilingualism. *Young Children* 72(2), 38–44.

Rasinski, T., & Zutell, J. (2010). *Essential strategies for word study: Effective methods for improving decoding, spelling, and vocabulary.* New York, NY: Scholastic.

Ravachew, S. (2010). Language development and literacy: Synthesis. In R. E. Tremblay, M. Boivin, R. D. V. Peters, & S. Rvachew (Eds.), *Encyclopedia on early childhood development.* Retrieved from www.child-encyclopedia.com/language-development-and-literacy/synthesis

Raver, C. C. (2002). Emotions matter: Making the case for the role of young children's emotional development for early school readiness. *SRCD Social Policy Report, XVI,* 3–18.

Rogoff, B. (2003). *The cultural nature of human development.* New York, NY: Oxford University Press.

Sampson, R. J., Sharkey, P., & Raudenbush, S. W. (2007). Durable effects of concentrated disadvantage on verbal ability among African-American children. *PNAS Early Edition,* 1–8. Retrieved from www.pnas.org_cgi_doi_10.1073_pnas.0710189104

Sesma, H. W., Mahone, M. E., Levine, T., Eason, S. H., & Cutting, L. E. (2009). The contribution of executive skills to reading comprehension. *Child Neuropsychology, 15*(3), 232–246.

Shonkoff, J. P. (2017). Breakthrough impacts: What science tells us about supporting early childhood development. *Young Children,* 72(2), 8–16.

Shonkoff, J. P., Garner, A. S., The Committee on Psychosocial Aspects of Child and Family Health, Committee on Early Childhood, Adoption, and Dependent Care, and Section on Developmental and Behavioral Pediatrics, Siegel, B. S., Dobbins, M. I., Earls, M. F., Garner, A. S., McGuinn, L., Pascoe, J., & Wood, D. L. (2012). Technical report of the American Academy of Pediatrics: The lifelong effects of early childhood adversity and toxic stress. *Pediatrics, 129*(1). Retrieved from pediatrics.aappublications.org/content/129/1/e232

Shonkoff, J. P., & Phillips, D. A. (Eds.). (2000). *From neurons to neighborhoods: The science of early childhood development.* Washington, DC: National Academy Press.

Siegel, D. J. (2001). Toward an interpersonal neurobiology of the developing mind: Attachment relationships, "mindsight," and neural integration. *Infant Mental Health Journal, 22*(1–2), 67–94.

Singer, D., Golinkoff, R. M., & Hirsh-Pasek, K. (Eds.). (2006). *Play = learning: How play motivates and enhances children's cognitive and social-emotional growth.* New York, NY: Oxford University Press.

Snow, C. E. (1983). Literacy and language: Relationships during the preschool years. *Harvard Educational Review, 53*(2), 165–189.

Snow, C. E., Burns, M. S., & Griffin, P. (1998). *Preventing reading difficulties in young children.* Washington, DC: National Academies Press.

Souto-Manning, M. (2013). *Multicultural teaching in the early childhood classroom: Approaches, strategies and tools, preschool–2nd grade.* New York, NY: Teachers College Press.

Souto-Manning, M., Falk, B., Lopez, D., Cardwell, N., Rabadi, A., Rollins, E., . . . Kim, H. (in press). A transdisciplinary approach to changing inequitable teaching practices in pre-K. *Review of Research in Education.*

Stipek, D. (2002). *Motivation to learn: Integrating theory and practice* (4th ed.). Boston, MA: Allyn & Bacon.

Suggate, S. P. (2012). Watering the garden before the rainstorm: The case of early reading. In S. Suggate & E. Reese (Eds.), *Contemporary debates in child development and education* (pp. 181–190). Abingdon, UK: Routledge/Taylor & Francis.

Teale, W., & Sulzby, E. (1986). *Emergent literacy: Writing and reading.* Westport, CT: Ablex Publishing.

Trentacosta, C. J., & Izard, C. E. (2007). Kindergarten children's emotion competence as a predictor of their academic competence in first grade. *Emotion 7*(1), 77.

United Nations. (2006). *Report of the independent expert for the United Nations study on violence against children.* New York, NY: Author.

Valdés, G. (1996). *Con respeto: Bridging the distances between culturally diverse families and schools: An ethnographic portrait.* New York, NY: Teachers College Press.

Viadero, D. (2007). Social-skills programs found to yield gains in academic subjects. *Education Week, 27*(16), 1, 15.

Vygotsky, L. (1966/1977). Play and its role in the mental development of the child. In M. Cole (Ed.), *Soviet developmental psychology* (pp. 76–99). Armonk, NY: M. E. Sharpe.

Wax, M. L., Wax, R. H., & Dumont, R. V., Jr. (1964). Formal education in an American Indian community. *Supplement to Social Problems* (Whole No. 1). Kalamazoo, MI: Society for the Study of Social Problems.

Weber, L. (1991). *Inquiry, noticing, joining with and following after.* New York, NY: Workshop Center, The City College of New York.

Weizman, Z. O., & Snow, C. E. (2001). Lexical output as related to children's vocabulary acquisition: Effects of sophisticated exposure and support for meaning. *Developmental Psychology, 37*(2), 265–279.

Willingham, D. (2017). *The reading mind: A cognitive approach to understanding how the mind reads.* San Francisco, CA: Jossey-Bass.

Zigler, E. F., Singer, D. G., & Bishop-Josef, S. J. (Eds.). (2004). *Children's play: The roots of reading.* Washington, DC: Zero to Three.

Index

The letter *f* after a page number refers to a figure.

About the Author

Beverly Falk is professor and director of the graduate programs in early childhood education at the School of Education of the City College of New York. She has served in a variety of educational roles—classroom teacher, early childhood center director, public school founder and principal, district administrator, researcher, and consultant—at the school, district, state, and national level. Her scholarship centers on early childhood education, teacher research, teacher education, and performance assessment. Throughout her career, her work has focused on supporting understandings about how children learn so as to ensure that our youngest, most vulnerable citizens—especially those from diverse, historically underserved, urban communities—have access to high-quality learning opportunities. Toward that end she has created the *High Quality Early Learning Project*, a web-based resource that shares videos of what high-quality teaching practices look like for young children: highqualityearlylearning.org.

The founding editor of *The New Educator*, a quarterly peer-reviewed journal about educator preparation, Dr. Falk is the author of numerous publications. Her books include *Defending Childhood: Keeping the Promise of Early Education* (Teachers College Press, 2012); *Teaching Matters: Stories from Inside City Schools,* coauthored with Megan Blumenreich (The New Press, 2012); *Teaching the Way Children Learn* (Teachers College Press, 2008); *The Power of Questions: A Guide to Teacher and Student Research,* coauthored with Megan Blumenreich (Heinemann, 2005); *The Heart of the Matter: Using Standards and Assessments to Learn*, (Heinemann, 2000); and *Authentic Assessment in Action*, coauthored with Linda Darling-Hammond and Jacqueline Ancess (Teachers College Press, 1997).